The Corner Hou

Sarah & D

PS Don't know much about this
cook book, but as it was
written by our first nation resident
thought you might Enjoy

# Kooking with a Koori

Kindest Regards

Liddy   2022

Australia

# Kooking with a Koori

## Budget-friendly recipes from TikTok star
**Nathan Lyons**

**SIMON &
SCHUSTER**

London · New York · Sydney · Toronto · New Delhi

KOOKING WITH A KOORI
First published in Australia in 2021 by
Simon & Schuster (Australia) Pty Limited
Suite 19A, Level 1, Building C, 450 Miller Street,
Cammeray, NSW 2062

10 9 8 7 6 5 4 3 2 1

Sydney New York London Toronto New Delhi
Visit our website at www.simonandschuster.com.au

© Nathan Lyons and Pamela Jones 2021

A catalogue record for this
book is available from the
National Library of Australia

ISBN: 9781761102011
Cover, internal design and illustrations: Meng Koach
Cover image: Lawrence Furzey
Printed and bound in Australia by Griffin Press

The paper this book is printed on is
certified against the Forest Stewardship
Council® Standards. Griffin Press
holds chain of custody certification
SGSHK–COC–005088. FSC® promotes
environmentally responsible, socially
beneficial and economically viable
management of the world's forests.

*This is for the communities: Indigenous, online, local, hobbies and the mob. Without y'all this would not have been possible.*

# Contents

# Introduction

'Ey welcome back to *Kooking with a Koori*. I'm Nathan Lyons and I'll be helping you make some madfeedz. I'm a dad, married with 6 kids that I know of and this is my story.

I grew up in the Sydney inner west suburbs of Glebe and Tempe. I have an older sister and 2 younger brothers. Raised by a single mum from about the age of 10 in housing commission, the dollar was tight so we had to learn how to make the money stretch. From an early age I was taught how to make cheap meals by Mum and Dad.

I remember going to shop at Jewel supermarket at Marrickville Metro. It's where the love of devon started – devon, cheese and tomato sauce sandwiches for school lunches. Growing up, Mum had a rule that the chef doesn't wash up, so I made sure I was the cook. When I was about 7 years old I started baking cakes for the family to enjoy. Secretly I used to love eating the leftover batter and icing by myself.

I have vivid memories of my nan teaching me how to make scrambled eggs and my aunties making cookies, chicken curry, curried eggs and Weet–Bix with powdered milk. My uncles showed me how to cook up a storm on a budget that'd impress Scrooge.

In my teens I adopted a second family with Hungarian and New Zealand heritage. There, I was shown a whole new world of cuisine. I learnt to love baked pumpkin and was introduced to eastern European recipes such as paprika cucumbers and sauerkraut. When Mumma Porkers made "chicken in pyjamas" (*chicken parmigiana*) the word would get out and I think I counted 20 there on one night.

I went to high school at Glebe High, where I met my wife, Krystal. I'd take her on after–school dates at Clem's Chicken in Newtown for gravy with a side of chips and then walk her home. I enjoy cooking for her and making her favourites. We never really planned on having a big family, but now we have 6 fussy eaters.

I uploaded my first food TikTok in September 2020, and it's grown from there. Not in my wildest dreams would I have thought it would lead me to where I am today, and for that I'm extremely grateful.

People ask what my plans are, and my reply is I don't have any. I'm just riding the wave of popularity and if that ends tomorrow, I'm fine with that. It's taken me on an amazing journey and one that I'm thankful for.

# Devon Delights

Devon is life. Devon has been an important part of modern Indigenous culture for at least 4 generations. Being a cheap meat and being so versatile, it has been a favourite in the community.

It's also known as fritz in South Australia, polony in Western Australia and luncheon meat in New Zealand. Communities across Australia and New Zealand will relate to these meals.

# Devon Curry

**Serves: 4 to 6**

*A simple yet delicious curry that can be made quickly in a pan or in the slow cooker and tastes even better the next day on toast. Best part is you can add your favourite vegetables.*

1kg devon roll
2 tablespoons vegetable oil
Curry powder, to taste
2 tablespoons plain flour
3 cups milk
420g can condensed cream of chicken and corn soup
1 cup frozen peas, corn and carrot

## Method:

- Cut devon into ½cm thick slices.
- Heat oil in a large frypan and fry up devon until browned.
- Throw in ya curry and flour, cook, stirring for 1 minute.
- Slowly pour in milk and soup, stirring until mixture boils and thickens.
- Toss in the vegies and bring to a boil. Simmer for 3 minutes.
- Season with salt and pepper.

*Serve with rice and have some madfeedz.*

*I use about 2 tablespoons Keen's curry powder in this recipe for a hot curry. Just use whatever amount you like.*

# Devon Toasties

**Makes: 2**

*A quick and easy snack for breakfast or dinner. Chuck on your favourite sauces and you'll be having some madfeedz in no time!*

4 slices white bread
Softened butter
4 large slices devon
Tomato sauce
2 cheese slices

**Method:**
• Butter bread slices on one side.
• Lay one slice of devon on each piece of bread.
• Squeeze tomato sauce over two of the devon slices, then top with cheese.
• Place remaining devon and bread on top.
• Toast sandwiches in a sandwich press or jaffle maker.

*Serve sprinkled with curry powder and topped with tomato sauce.*

> *You can use devon that's already sliced from the deli counter. We love harvarti sliced cheese in these toasties. Use your favourite cheese – tasty or Swiss tastes great, too.*

# Devon Steaks

**Makes: about 12**

*A quick and easy snack on its own or thrown together with other things to make a meal. Change the seasonings to create new flavours.*

500g devon roll
Olive oil
Chicken salt
Freshly ground pepper

**Method:**
• Cut devon roll into 1cm thick slices.
• Drizzle over some olive oil and rub over slices.
• Sprinkle both sides of devon with chicken salt and pepper.
• Cook in a sandwich press or frypan until golden brown on both sides.

*Serve on buttered toast with sliced cheese and tomato sauce.*

**TIP**

1kg devon rolls *(also known as knobs of devon)* can be found in the refrigerator section of supermarkets or in delicatessens. This recipe uses half a 1kg roll.

# Devon Pizza

**Makes: 1**

*A fantastic one to get the kids involved! Use ready–made bases from the store or start from scratch. So many different combinations – the choice is yours.*

100g devon roll
1 large pizza base
¼ cup tomato paste
1 teaspoon minced garlic
1 cup shredded pizza cheese
½ cup canned pineapple pieces

## Method:

• Cut devon roll into ½cm slices. Cut into wedge–shaped pieces.
• Place pizza base on a greased tray.
• Spread tomato paste over pizza base, then spread over garlic.
• Sprinkle cheese over base.
• Top with devon and well–drained pineapple pieces.
• Cook pizza in oven at 190ºC for about 13 to 15 minutes or until cheese is melted and base is crisp.

# Koori Snack Pack

**Serves: 2 to 4**

*A Koori version of a popular snack pack you'd buy from the local kebab shop. Cook your own chips or buy some fresh hot chips. Add your favourite sauces then boom: #MADFEEDZ!*

Medium box of fresh hot chips
1 tablespoon oil
125g shaved devon
1½ cups grated tasty cheese

**Method:**
- Place chips on a flameproof plate or oven tray.
- Heat oil in a frypan, fry up devon until lightly browned.
- Chuck the hot devon on the chips.
- Sprinkle over cheese. Place under a hot grill or in a 190°C oven to melt the cheese.

*Serve with tomato or barbecue sauce. Awwww deadly!*

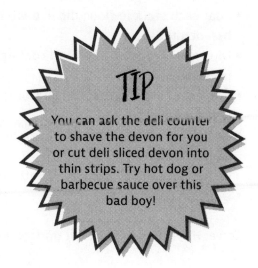

TIP

You can ask the deli counter to shave the devon for you or cut deli sliced devon into thin strips. Try hot dog or barbecue sauce over this bad boy!

# Devon Schnitzels

**Makes: 4**

*Once you have this essential down pat you can add it into so many other meals. The layered cheese melts between the devon and the fried bread crumbs give a delicious crunch.*

16 large slices devon
12 slices cheddar or tasty cheese
4 eggs
Plain flour, to coat
Dried breadcrumbs, to coat
Vegetable oil, for deep frying

**Method:**
- Layer 4 devon slices and 3 cheese slices starting with a devon slice, then a cheese slice until you have a devon slice on top and a nice layered stack. Repeat with remaining devon and cheese to make four stacks.
- Use an egg ring or large round scone cutter to cut the stacks into a round cake shape.
- Lightly beat eggs in a bowl.
- Coat each stack in flour, dip in beaten eggs, then in breadcrumbs.
- Dip again in beaten eggs and coat again in breadcrumbs, pressing on firmly.
- Cover and place in the refrigerator for about 30 minutes or until you are ready to cook.
- Heat oil in a large, deep saucepan or deep fryer over a medium heat.
- Cook schnitzels one at a time until golden brown all over.
- Drain on paper towel.

*Serve with salad or go all out and serve with chips and gravy.*

# Devon Spaghetti Bolognese

**Serves: 4**

 *A family favourite in any household. Add in some of your personal favourite vegies and serve with garlic bread. Deadly!*

500g devon roll
2 tablespoons olive oil
2 teaspoons dried Italian seasoning
½ cup grated tasty cheese
500g jar pasta sauce
400g spaghetti, cooked

## Method:

• Cut devon into pieces. Finely chop in a food processor or coarsely grate.
• Heat oil in a large frypan over medium heat and fry that devon for 2 minutes.
• Chuck in Italian seasoning and cheese, cook, stirring for 1 minute.
• Pour in the pasta sauce and simmer for 2 to 3 minutes. The sauce will become a paste like consistency. *(Don't worry, its taste will be on point!)*

*Serve with cooked spaghetti and extra grated cheese.*

*Your local butcher may be able to mince the devon for you. Otherwise grated devon works, too.*

# Devon & Cheese Balls

**Makes: about 30**

*A Koori twist on a family favourite. Get the kids involved and have some fun making these. Serve at a party or anytime!*

400g devon roll
110g tub pitted Kalamata olives
200g cream cheese
100g grated cheddar cheese
50g grated parmesan cheese

**Method:**
- Finely chop devon and olives. Place in a bowl.
- Chop cream cheese into small pieces. Add to devon and olives and mix well. Season with salt and pepper.
- Add cheddar and parmesan cheese and mix until combined.
- Form mixture into small balls. Cover and place in refrigerator until firm.

*To fancy these up, roll in chopped parsley or chives.*

# Devon Sausage Rolls

**Makes: 18**

*A delicious feed that the kids can get involved in, making dinner or lunch box treats for school.*

1kg devon roll
1 small onion
2 cloves garlic
2 teaspoons smoked paprika
1 teaspoon fennel seeds
1 teaspoon ground cumin
½ teaspoon ground black pepper
1 egg
1 tablespoon milk
3 sheets frozen ready rolled puff pastry, thawed

**Method:**
• Coarsely grate devon using a cheese grater. *(A food processor will also do the job.)* Place in a large bowl.
• Peel onion and garlic and finely chop.
• Throw the onion, garlic and spices in with the devon and mix well.
• Whisk egg and milk together.
• Cut each pastry sheet in half and spread devon mixture along the centre of each sheet in a long sausage shape.
• Brush one long side of pastry with egg mix. Roll up to enclose
• Using a sharp knife, cut each roll into three pieces. Place seam side down onto an oven tray lined with baking paper.
• Brush rolls with egg mixture. Cook in oven at 200°C for 20 minutes then lower oven temperature to 180°C for a further 10 minutes or until golden brown.

*Serve with tomato sauce.*

# Devon Tortilla Wrap
**Makes: 1**

*A Koori take on a viral TikTok video that you can change up with your favourite ingredients. Toasted or straight up, they both taste great.*

1 large tortilla or wrap
4 large slices devon
2 slices tomato
2 slices cheese
Tomato sauce

**Method:**
- Lay your tortilla on a chopping board and make a cut from the middle of the tortilla down to the edge.
- Imagine the tortilla being divided up into four quadrants or quarters.
- Place 2 devon slices into one quadrant, 2 cheese slices into another quadrant, 2 tomato slices into third quadrant and 2 slices devon in remaining quadrant.
- Squeeze tomato sauce over devon.
- Fold the wrap up, starting from the bottom left cut quarter, folding it up over the top left, then folding it over to the top right, then folding it down to the bottom right. You should now have a thick wedge–shaped tortilla.

*To serve, cook in a sandwich press or frypan until golden and crisp.*

# Creamy Potato Devon Bake

**Serves: 4 to 6**

*Always a favourite at any get–together. This popular potato dish layered with devon will feed a crowd and have them lining up for seconds!*

6 large potatoes
1 onion
2 cloves garlic
12 thin devon slices
1½ cups thickened cream
½ cup chicken stock

## METHOD:

• Peel potatoes and onion and thinly slice.
• Peel and crush the garlic.
• Roughly chop the devon.
• Layer potatoes, onion and devon in a greased ovenproof dish *(10 cup capacity)* repeating layers twice.
• Place cream, chicken stock and garlic in a large saucepan.
• Bring to a simmer, season with salt and pepper. Pour evenly over potato mixture.
• Cook in oven at 180°C for 1 to 1¼ hours or until potatoes are very tender.
• Set aside for 5 to 10 minutes to cool slightly before serving the mob this mad feed.

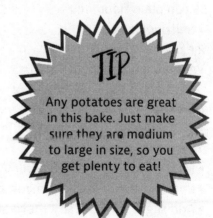

**TIP**

Any potatoes are great in this bake. Just make sure they are medium to large in size, so you get plenty to eat!

# Sweet & Sour Crispy Devon

**Serves: 4**

*A Koori version of an Asian classic. Sweet and sour sauce with anything crispy just can't be beaten! You can add your favourite vegies.*

**Sweet & Sour Sauce**
1 green capsicum
1 carrot
1 tablespoon oil
½ teaspoon minced garlic
½ cup caster sugar
½ cup white vinegar
1 tablespoon soy sauce
2 tablespoons cornflour
425g can pineapple pieces in natural juices, drained

**Crispy Devon**
500g devon roll
½ cup cornflour
⅓ cup plain flour
1 teaspoon salt
2 eggs
Vegetable oil, to deep fry

**Method:**
- To make sauce, cut capsicum into 3cm pieces. Peel and slice carrot thinly.
- Heat oil in a large saucepan over medium heat. Chuck in the capsicum, carrot and garlic, stir fry for 3 minutes.
- Add sugar, vinegar, soy sauce and 1 cup water, stirring until sugar dissolves.
- Mix cornflour with 2 tablespoons water until smooth. Gradually add to sauce, stirring constantly until sauce boils and thickens. Simmer for 2 minutes. Stir in pineapple. Keep warm.

- To make Crispy Devon, chop devon into 3cm pieces.
- In a bowl, whisk together cornflour, plain flour, salt, eggs and 2 tablespoons water, to make a thick batter. Add more water if needed.
- Coat devon pieces in the batter.
- Heat oil in a large deep saucepan or deep fryer over a medium heat. Deep fry devon pieces in batches for 2 to 3 minutes or until golden brown and crispy. Remove from pan and drain on paper towel.
- Stir devon gently through sauce or serve devon on top of sauce to keep crispy.

*Serve with rice.*

# Devon Cake

*A cheeky and creative way to serve devon for that devon–obsessed person in the mob. Take it a step further and dust some curry powder on it.*

Devon slices
Cheese slices
Thick smooth cold mashed potato
Cream cheese spread

**Method:**
- Layer devon and cheese slices until desired height is reached, about 3 to 4cm high is good.
- Push down an egg ring or round cutter to create a uniform smooth circle.
- Use mash as an icing to coat the side and top of cake.
- Place in the refrigerator until mash is firm.
- Place cheese spread into a piping bag and pipe around edge on top of the cake to create a decorative ring.

# Devon Garlic Butter Rice

**Serves: 2 to 3**

 *No bread here! This ricey twist on garlic bread makes a perfect side dish for so many things.*

100g devon roll
90g butter
1 cup long grain white rice
2 tablespoons minced garlic
2 chicken stock cubes
3 cups chicken stock
1 teaspoon curry powder *(optional)*

## Method:

• Chop devon into 1 to 2cm pieces.
• Melt butter in a frypan over medium heat.
• Throw in the devon, fry up until golden.
• Chuck in the rice and garlic, cook stirring for 1 to 2 minutes or until garlic and rice starts to change colour.
• Toss in the stock cubes, stir until softened.
• Pour in the stock, stir well. *(If adding curry, now's the time.)*
• Simmer gently for 10 minutes or until rice is almost tender and most, but not all, of the stock/butter mixture has been absorbed. Stir gently.
• Cover pan with lid and cook for 5 more minutes or until rice is cooked and all of the liquid has been absorbed. *(If there is still some melted butter at the bottom of the pan, that's okay.)*

*Serve sprinkled with cheese or chopped chives.*

# Slow Cooker Devon Ragu

**Serves: 4**

*A beautiful meal for a cold winter's night.*

1kg devon roll
1 large onion
2 carrots
2 stalks celery
2 tablespoons olive oil
1 cup dry red wine
2 x 400g cans cherry tomatoes in juice
1 cup beef stock
2 tablespoons tomato paste
3 sprigs fresh thyme

**Method:**
• Chop devon into 3cm pieces.
• Peel and finely chop onion and carrots.
• Finely chop celery.
• Heat oil in ya large frypan over a high heat.
• Fry up devon in two batches for 4 to 5 minutes or until browned.
  Transfer to bowl of a 5 litre slow cooker.
• Toss all the other ingedients into the slow cooker, mix well.
  Cover with lid.
• Cook on Low for 6 hours or on High for 4 hours. Remove thyme
  stalks and discard. Season with salt and pepper.

*Serve with cooked fettucine, chopped parsley and grated parmesan.*

# Chinese Cabbage with Chilli, Devon & Garlic

**Serves: 2**

*A delicious, light meal with amazing flavours.*

100g devon roll
¼ Chinese cabbage
2 dried red chillies
2 cloves garlic
1 teaspoon cornflour
2 tablespoons oil
1 tablespoon soy sauce
1 tablespoon black vinegar or rice wine vinegar
1 teaspoon sugar

**Method:**
• Chop devon into 1cm pieces.
• Chop cabbage into 5cm pieces.
• Cut chillies into 1cm lengths. Peel and roughly chop garlic.
• Mix together cornflour and 2 tablespoons water until smooth.
• Heat a wok or large frypan over a high heat. Chuck in the oil, devon, chillies and garlic and stir fry for 30 secs.
• Toss cabbage in and stir fry for 1 minute.
• Pour in soy sauce, vinegar and sugar, stir fry 30 seconds.
• Drizzle in the cornflour mixture, stirring until liquid in the wok boils, thickens and coats the cabbage.

*Serve with rice.*

# Devon, Cheese & Tomato Omelette

**Serves: 1**

*A quick and easy meal for any time of the day.*

1 smallish tomato

2 eggs

1 tablespoon milk

2 teaspoons butter

1 tablespoon grated parmesan

1 tablespoon grated cheddar cheese

1 tablespoon finely chopped chives or parsley

2 large slices devon

## Method:

• Cut the tomato in half, remove seeds with a teaspoon. Finely chop tomato.

• In a bowl, beat eggs and milk together with a fork. Season with salt and pepper.

• Melt butter in a frypan over low to medium heat. Pour in egg mixture and cook until the underside of omelette is golden.

• Lower heat and sprinkle over cheeses, chives and diced tomato. Lay devon slices on one half of omelette.

• Cook for a further 30 seconds to 1 minute or until egg is cooked, then slide omelette from the pan onto a plate, folding the omelette in half.

*Serve with buttered toast.*

# Italian-Style Devon Bake

**Serves: 4 to 6**

*Pesto is an instant flavour booster and makes everything taste like you've been slaving away for hours. Prepare this dish a few hours ahead and leave in fridge. When ready to cook, pour in stock and bake.*

500g devon roll
6 cloves garlic
6 potatoes
190g jar sundried tomato pesto
2 tablespoons olive oil
1 cup chicken stock
1 cup grated parmesan cheese
2 punnets cherry tomatoes

## Method:

- Cut devon into 2cm thick slices, cut slices into quarters. Place in a large baking dish.
- Peel and halve garlic.
- Wash or peel potatoes and cut into thin wedges, toss into the dish with garlic.
- Add pesto and oil, using your hands toss everything together. Sprinkle generously with salt and pepper.
- Pour chicken stock into corner of pan *(not over the top)*.
- Cook in a hot oven *(200ºC)* for 50 minutes or until potatoes are light golden and almost cooked, turning once during cooking.
- Remove from oven. Arrange tomatoes over top, sprinkle over parmesan.
- Return to oven for a further 15 minutes or until parmesan and potatoes are golden brown.

*Serve with lemon wedges and a green salad or fresh crusty bread to mop up the pan juices.*

# Potato-Topped Devon Pie

**Serves: 4**

*Make your own mash if you like.*

500g knob devon
1 large onion
300g mushrooms
¼ cup traditional gravy powder
2 tablespoons oil
1½ cups frozen peas, carrot and corn
2 sheets frozen shortcrust pastry, thawed
475g tub classic potato mash
1 cup grated tasty cheese

## Method:

- Chop devon into 1 to 2cm pieces.
- Peel onion and chop finely. Slice mushrooms.
- Mix together gravy powder and ½ cup boiling water.
- Heat oil in a large frying pan over medium heat. Cook onion and mushrooms for 5 minutes or until softened.
- Throw in devon, gravy mix and frozen vegies and bring to a boil, cook stirring for 1 minute. Remove from heat.
- Cut sheets of pastry to line the base and sides of a 20cm greased ovenproof pie dish, joining pastry by pressing firmly together.
- Cook in oven at 200°C for about 20 minutes or until light golden.
- Spoon pie filling into pastry base. Top with spoonfuls of potato mash and sprinkle with cheese.
- Return to oven for a further 15 minutes or until cheese is golden brown.

*Serve with tomato sauce of course!*

# Devon & Pickled Onion Salad

**Serves: 4**

*Looks a bit different, but this salad tastes damn good. Use your favourite dressing.*

150g jar cocktail onions
½ cup Ranch or Thousand Island dressing
½ iceberg or cos lettuce
1 large green capsicum
200g sliced devon
1 punnet cherry tomatoes
1 large avocado
2 cups corn chips

## Method:

- To make dressing, add 2 tablespoons liquid from cocktail onion jar to bottled dressing. Season with salt and pepper.
- Tear or slice lettuce into chunks. Place into a large salad bowl.
- Slice capsicum and devon into strips, add to bowl.
- Halve cherry tomatoes and cocktail onions, add to bowl.
- To serve, cut avocados into small chunks and scatter over salad.
- Drizzle some of the dressing over salad and gently toss.
- Top with corn chips.

*Serve with remaining dressing.*

# Spicy Spanish Rice

**Serves: 4**

*The crust is what makes this rice taste so good. Keep an eye on it towards the end of cooking time so it doesn't burn. If it's not crusty enough, cook a bit longer.*

250g devon roll
1 chorizo *(optional)*
1 large onion
330g jar whole roasted peppers
2 tablespoons olive oil
2 teaspoons smoked paprika
1½ cups medium grain white rice
140g tub tomato paste
2 chicken stock cubes
2 cups sliced fresh beans or frozen peas

## Method:

- Cut devon into 1cm thick slices, then cut slices into quarters.
- Cut chorizo into ½cm slices, then cut slices into small pieces.
- Peel onion and chop finely. Drain peppers, cut into 2cm pieces.
- Heat oil in a large frypan. Chuck in the onion and cook until slightly softened.
- Toss in the devon, chorizo and paprika and fry until chorizo and devon are lightly browned.
- Add the peppers, rice, tomato paste, stock cubes and 3 cups water. Stir and bring to the boil.
- Lower heat, cover with lid and simmer for about 15 to 20 minutes or until most of liquid is absorbed and rice has made a nice golden brown crust on base of pan.

# Devon Croquettes

*A Koori version of a classic deep fried delight. Fantastic to eat straight away as a main or a snack or saved for lunch.*

Large devon roll
Swiss cheese slices
Eggs
Plain flour, to coat
Dried breadcrumbs, to coat
Vegetable oil, for deep frying

**Method:**
- Cut a 2 to 3cm thick slice from devon roll. Using a small knife, carve out a cavity in the slice, don't cut all the way through.
- Fill the cavity with chopped, crushed Swiss cheese.
- Cut a thin slice from devon roll and chop or squash to seal the cavity. Repeat to make as many croquettes as you want.
- Lightly beat eggs in a bowl.
- Coat croquettes in flour, then dip in beaten eggs, then in breadcrumbs.
- Dip again in the eggs and coat again in the breadcrumbs, pressing on firmly.
- Place in refrigerator until ready to cook.
- Heat oil in a large, deep saucepan or deep fryer over a medium heat.
- Add croquettes, one or two at a time and deep fry until golden brown all over.
- Drain on paper towel.

*Serve as part of a burger or just on its own with tomato sauce.*

# Pigs in Blankets

*They are known as many things across Australia, however one thing everyone agrees on is they are a party essential. Make the mash your way, add sauce if you like, then you'll be as happy as a pig in a blanket!*

Cooled mashed potato
Large slices of devon
Tomato sauce or tomato relish

**Method:**
• Make mashed potato your way.
• Spoon the mash along the centre of each slice of devon.
• Squeeze or spoon over your favourite sauce or relish.
• Roll up devon slice and place seam side down on plate or secure with a toothpick.

**TIP**

Use your favourite sauce or condiment here. We like mustard pickles and sweet chilli sauce. American squeeze mustard is good, too.

# Breakfast/ Brunch

Breakfast is often called "the most important meal of the day", and for good reason. As the name suggests, breakfast breaks the overnight fasting period. It replenishes your supply of glucose to boost your energy levels and alertness, while also providing other essential nutrients required for good health.

# Egg in a Hole

**Serves: 1**

*An old family favourite of mine that I enjoyed as a kid, and now mine enjoy it, too.*

1 slice of your favourite kind of bread
1 tablespoon butter
1 egg

## Method:

- Using a biscuit cutter or the rim of a glass, punch out a hole in the centre of the slice of bread.
- Melt butter in a frypan over low to medium heat.
- Place bread in the pan and crack the egg into the centre of the hole.
- Cook until the egg sets slightly on the base, about 1 to 1½ minutes. Season with salt and pepper.
- Turn the egg over with a spatula.
- Move the toast around in the skillet, soaking up all of the glorious butter. Cook until the yolk is done as you like it.

*Here's the key: golden brown toast, white egg whites (not browned or burned), soft unbroken yolk. Perfect!*

# Breakfast Burritos

**Serves: 4**

 *The best breakfast burrito recipe is the one that you create! The possibilities are limitless and they are the perfect size so you can eat on the run.*

4 flour tortillas
1 tomato
350g chopped ham, sausage or bacon
8 eggs
½ cup milk
1 tablespoon olive oil
1⅓ cups shredded cheese

## Method:

• Warm tortillas in oven, microwave or in a dry frypan over low heat *(follow packet directions)*.
• Meanwhile, slice the tomato.
• Chop ham, sausage or bacon into 1 to 2cm pieces.
• Whisk eggs and milk together in a bowl. Season with salt and pepper.
• Heat oil in a large frypan, add ham, sausage or bacon, cook over medium heat until browned. Remove meat from the pan and set aside.
• If using sausage or bacon, drain oil from pan leaving a small amount in the pan for cooking the eggs.
• Pour the egg mixture into pan, cook stirring until eggs start to set.
• Sprinkle in the ham, sausage or bacon.
• Continue stirring until eggs are cooked. Remove from heat, sprinkle over cheese.
• Divide between the 4 tortillas and top with sliced tomato.
• Roll each tortilla into a burrito and serve.

# Banana Pancakes

**Serves: 6**

 *You will need about 3 medium bananas here.*

1 cup white or wholemeal flour
¼ cup sugar
1 teaspoon bicarb soda
¼ teaspoon salt
1½ cups buttermilk
1 egg
½ teaspoon vanilla extract
½ cup mashed banana
1 to 2 bananas, sliced

## Method:

• Mix flour, sugar, bicarb soda and salt together in a large bowl.
• In a separate bowl, whisk buttermilk, egg and vanilla extract together.
• Pour buttermilk mixture into dry ingredients, stir until well combined.
• Stir in mashed banana, mix well.
• Heat a lightly greased frypan over a medium heat. Pour ¼ to ⅓ cup of batter into pan.
• Place a few banana slices on top of the pancake.
• Cook pancakes for 1 to 2 minutes or until bubbles form on surface and base is golden brown.
• Turn over, cook a further 1 to 1½ minutes or until golden brown on both sides. Repeat with remaining batter, stacking pancakes on a plate as they are cooked.

*Serve with butter and hot maple syrup.*

# Foolproof Eggs Benedict

**Serves: 3**

*Master this iconic breakfast recipe and you will have a crowd lining up outside your place! I use mugs to lower the eggs into the water – you do whatever works for you.*

6 large eggs
2 tablespoons white vinegar
6 slices ham or bacon
3 English muffins
Fresh chopped chives or parsley, to serve

**Hollandaise Sauce**
250g unsalted butter
3 large egg yolks
1 tablespoon fresh lemon juice

**Method:**
- To poach eggs, fill a large saucepan three quarters full with water.
- Tip in the vinegar and 1 teaspoon salt and bring to a boil over high heat.
- Crack the eggs into coffee mugs, 2 in each cup.
- Reduce the water to a simmer. Lower the rims of the mugs into the water and gently tip the eggs into the pan one mug at a time as quickly as you can.
- Bring water back to a simmer for 1 minute.
- Remove the pan from heat, cover and leave eggs to poach for 5 to 6 minutes.

- Meanwhile, cook the ham or bacon in a large, lightly oiled frypan over medium heat until browned on both sides (like me). Keep warm.
- Split muffins in half and toast.
- Meanwhile, make Hollandaise Sauce *(prepare just before serving)*.
- Melt butter in a small saucepan over a low heat.
- Place egg yolks and lemon juice together in a blender, blend until smooth and frothy, about 10 seconds.
- With blender running, very slowly drizzle in the warm butter until all butter is added and sauce is thickened. Season with salt and pepper.
- To serve, place muffin halves on plates, top with ham or bacon.
- Gently remove eggs from water with a slotted spoon, place poached eggs onto muffin halves.
- Pour hollandaise sauce over eggs and garnish with chives or parsley.

*Enjoy some madfeedz!*

# Easy Breakfast Bake

**Serves: 8**

*This breakfast bake is an awesome way to start the day! You start off with simple ingredients like eggs, hash browns and cheese. After that, you can dress this up a million ways. Add different meats and vegies to create a fun morning meal your whole family will enjoy.*

1 red capsicum
1 onion
500g frozen hash browns
300g pork mince
2 cups shredded cheddar cheese
12 eggs
1 cup milk
1 teaspoon salt
½ teaspoon pepper

**Method:**
• Chop capsicum into 2cm pieces.
• Peel and chop onion into 1cm pieces.
• Break up frozen hash browns into shredded pieces, place in a large bowl.
• Heat a large frypan over medium heat. Throw in mince, capsicum and onion, cook until mince is browned, stirring to break up any lumps. Drain off any excess fat. Cool slightly.
• Chuck the mince mixture in with the hash browns, mix well. Stir in cheese.
• Spread mixture into a greased 23cm x 33cm baking dish.
• Whisk eggs, milk, salt and pepper together in a large bowl.
• Pour over the hash browns, vegies and mince.
• Cook in oven at 180°C for 50 to 60 minutes, or until eggs are set in the centre and don't jiggle.

# Cornflake-Coated Crispy Bacon

**Serves: 6**

*A delightful way to enjoy some oven roasted bacon, crispy as!*

½ cup evaporated milk
2 tablespoons tomato sauce
1 tablespoon Worcestershire sauce
18 strips streaky bacon
3 cups crushed cornflakes

## Method:

- Mix together milk, tomato sauce and Worcestershire sauce in a medium bowl. Season with pepper.
- Chuck in bacon strips, turning to coat them all over.
- Dip each bacon strip in crushed cornflakes, pressing to help the coating stick.
- Place 2 x greased wire racks into 2 x roasting pans. Lay bacon strips on racks.
- Cook in oven at 190°C for 25 to 30 minutes or until golden and crisp, rotating baking dishes halfway through cooking.

# Corn Fritters with Bacon, Roasted Tomatoes & Avocado Salsa

**Serves: 8**

*A lubly way to start a deadly day with some awesome fritters.*

## Roasted Tomatoes

4 small Roma tomatoes, halved
2 tablespoons olive oil
½ teaspoon dried mixed herbs
200g smoked bacon

## Avocado Salsa

2 ripe avocados
2 tablespoons lemon juice
2 spring onions
¼ cup chopped coriander leaves
1 teaspoon chilli paste *(optional)*

## Corn Fritters

1 red onion
2 eggs
¼ cup chopped coriander leaves
¾ cup plain flour
1 teaspoon baking powder
525g fresh corn kernels *(about 3 cobs)*
¼ cup vegetable oil
100g baby spinach leaves, to serve

## Method:

**To cook roasted tomatoes and bacon**

• Crank that oven to 180°C.
• Cut tomatoes in half lengthways. Place on a greased baking tray, cut side up.

- Drizzle with olive oil and season generously with salt and pepper. Sprinkle with dried herbs.
- Cook in oven for 20 to 30 minutes. In the last 10 minutes move the tomatoes to the bottom rack in oven and turn the grill on.
- Place bacon rashers onto grilling rack. Cook until crisp and crunchy on both sides. Remove bacon and tomatoes and keep warm.

### To make avocado salsa
- Remove seeds, peel and chop avocados into 2cm pieces. Place in a bowl and pour over lemon juice.
- Slice spring onions thinly, add to avocado with coriander and chilli paste *(if using)*, season with salt and pepper, gently mix together. Set aside.

### To make corn fritters
- Peel and chop onion into 2cm pieces.
- Chuck the onion, eggs, coriander, flour, baking powder and half the corn kernels in a food processor and process until almost smooth, about 30 seconds.
- Place in a large bowl, throw in the remaining corn, season with salt and pepper and mix well.
- Heat 1 tablespoon of the oil in a large non–stick frypan over a medium heat.
- Spoon 2 heaped tablespoons of mixture into pan and cook in several batches for 1 to 2 minutes each side or until golden brown and cooked in centre *(adding more oil to pan as needed)*.
- Drain on paper towel and keep warm.

### To serve
- Place fritters onto plates, add tomatoes, bacon and a handful of spinach leaves to each plate.
- Top fritters with avocado salsa.

# Cheesy Corn Toasties

**Serves: 3 to 4**

**CHEAP EATS**

*A quick and easy brekkie for a busy day ahead.*

2 to 3 spring onions
6 slices bread
1 large egg
½ cup creamed corn
1 cup shredded tasty cheese

**Method:**
- Finely chop spring onions.
- Toast bread until lightly brown.
- Mix egg, corn, cheese and spring onions in a bowl with a fork.
- Spread the mixture over the toast right to the edges *(to stop edges burning)*.
- Place under a grill, cook on medium heat *(not too close to heat)* until golden brown and bubbly.

# Easy Egg La Muffins

**Serves: 1**

 *Everyone loves the muffins from the golden arches. Here's my version for when the kids ask to go for one of them from that place.*

1 English muffin
Butter, to spread
1 tablespoon olive oil
1 large egg
1 slice bacon or ham
1 slice American or cheddar cheese
Cooking oil spray

**Method:**

- Slice muffin in half, toast and spread with butter.
- Heat oil in a frypan. Cook egg as you like it.
- If you want to get real deadly, cut the top off a tuna can, wash well and dry, then spray the inside well with cooking spray.
- Place can in the hot pan and break egg into it. Poke a hole in the yolk with a toothpick or skewer.
- Cook until the egg becomes white and firm. *(You can use an egg ring too – that would probably be easier.)* Remove from pan.
- Place slice of cheese on bottom half of muffin. Top with egg, keep warm.
- Return pan to heat, add bacon or ham and cook until browned on both sides.
- Place bacon onto egg and cover with the top of the toasted muffin. Lubly lah!

# Mini Meat Pies

**Makes: 24**

*A fantastic treat while watching the mighty Rabbitohs or for the lunch box.*

1 carrot
1 onion
2 cloves garlic
1 tablespoon oil
500g beef mince
¼ cup traditional gravy mix
2 sheets ready rolled shortcrust pastry, thawed
2 sheets ready rolled puff pastry, thawed
1 egg

**Method:**
- To make filling, peel carrot, coarsely grate.
- Peel onion and garlic and finely chop.
- Heat oil in a large frypan over medium heat. Throw in the onion and garlic and cook stirring for 2 minutes.
- Chuck in the mince and fry up until mince changes colour, stirring to break up any lumps.
- Toss in the carrot, mix well.
- In a heatproof jug, mix together gravy powder and 1 cup of boiling water until smooth. Gradually pour it into the mince mixture stirring over medium heat until sauce boils and thickens. Boil gently for 1 minute. Remove from heat, set aside to cool for 30 minutes.
- To assemble pies, cut shortcrust pastry sheets into 24 squares. Repeat with puff pastry sheets.
- Grease and line 2 x 12 hole mini muffin pans *(2 tablespoon capacity)* with shortcrust pastry squares.
- Spoon mince mixture into pastry cases.

- Top each case with a puff pastry square, pressing around edges to seal. Use a small sharp knife to trim away excess pastry.
- Brush top of pies with lightly beaten egg.
- Cook in oven at 180°C for 20 to 25 minutes or until golden brown.
- Cool pies in pans for 5 minutes then place on a wire rack.

*Serve pies with tomato sauce.*

# Vegemite & Avocado on Toast
**Serves: 2**

*A fresh and healthy breakfast to start smashing them KPIs at work.*

1 avocado
4 slices sourdough
Butter
Vegemite

**Method:**
- Remove seed, peel and slice avocado.
- Toast sourdough slices, spread with butter and vegemite.
- Top with avocado and serve.

# Honey Nut Bars

**Makes: 15**

*Three recipes in one! Try these honey bars in a delicious cranberry or peanut flavour by following the variations at the end of recipe.*

1 cup almonds
½ cup cashews
½ cup pecans
½ cup shredded or desiccated coconut
½ cup dark choc bits
1 teaspoon vanilla extract
¼ teaspoon mixed spice
¾ cup honey

**Method:**

- Grease a 19cm square cake pan, line base and sides with baking paper, allowing paper to overhang sides of pan slightly.
- Finely chop almonds, cashews and pecans. *(Pieces should be no bigger than 7 mm.)*
- Place nuts and all other ingredients except honey in a large bowl and stir well.
- Pour over the honey and mix with a fork until everything is very well coated.
- Spread mixture into prepared pan, pressing down well to reach all edges and corners of the pan. *(Use oiled hands to do this.)*
- Cook in the oven at 180°C for about 20 minutes. *(Watch carefully towards the end of cook time to make sure the honey isn't burning. It should be bubbly around the edges, though.)*
- Remove from the oven, place the pan onto a wire rack. Leave

until cool enough to handle but still quite warm, then use another piece of baking paper to press the top of slice down firmly. Cool for another 30 minutes.

• Place a new sheet of baking paper on the bench, lift the slice from pan, then turn over onto paper.

• Re–shape back into a square and press down. Peel off the baking paper.

• Allow to cool completely. Cut into 15 slices and wrap individually in baking paper to keep them from sticking together. Store in an airtight container in a cool place. Eat within 2 weeks.

## VARIATIONS:
### Cranberry and Nut Bars
Add ½ cup finely chopped dried cranberries or other finely chopped dried fruit. You can take out the choc bits if you like or leave them in.

### Peanut Bars
Add 1 tablespoon peanut butter and substitute ½ cup finely chopped roasted peanuts for the cashews.

# Pikelets

**Makes: about 18**

*These mini pancakes are sure to be a hit with the family. Serve with your favourite toppings – I reckon butter and jam and more jam!*

1 cup self raising flour
¼ teaspoon bicarb soda
¼ cup caster sugar
1 egg
¾ cup milk
1 tablespoon butter
Jam, whipped cream, to serve

**Method**
- Sift flour and soda together in a medium bowl.
- Stir in sugar. Make a well in centre.
- Lightly beat egg and milk together with a fork, stir into flour mixture to make a thick smooth batter with a pouring consistency. Rest 15 minutes.
- Heat a large, non-stick frypan over medium heat. Melt about 1 teaspoon of butter over the pan.
- Spoon tablespoons of batter into pan *(about 4 at a time)*, spacing each one apart, to allow for spreading.
- Cook 1 to 2 minutes or until bubbles appear on the surface and base of pikelet is golden brown.
- Turn and cook a further 1 minute or until golden brown on base. Remove from pan and stack on a plate. Continue cooking in batches adding butter to pan when needed.

# Mini Quiches

**Makes: 24**

*A great treat that can be changed to whatever you feel like, in our house we sometimes add devon instead of ham.*

½ small onion
80g ham
5 large eggs
½ cup cream
3 sheets ready rolled puff pastry, thawed
1 cup grated cheese

## Method:
• Grate onion. Chop ham into 1cm pieces.
• Place eggs, cream and onion in a bowl, season with salt and pepper, whisk together well.
• Cut pastry sheets into rounds to line 2 x greased 12 hole mini muffin pans *(2 tablespoon capacity)*.
• Divide ham and cheese into muffin holes. Pour or spoon in egg mixture to fill.
• Cook in oven at 200°C for 20 to 22 minutes until golden and crisp. Cool in pans for 5 minutes, then remove quiches and cool on a wire rack.

# Homemade Soft Pretzels
**Makes: 12**

 *A lovely recipe. With a bit of practice you will knock out some deadly pretzels.*

1½ cups warm water
2¼ teaspoons instant dried yeast
1 teaspoon salt
1 tablespoon brown sugar or white sugar
1 tablespoon melted butter
3–3½ cups plain flour
Coarse sea salt, for sprinkling

**Bicarb Soda Mix**
½ cup bicarb soda
2¼ litres water

**Method:**
- Whisk together warm water and yeast in a medium bowl. Allow to sit for 1 minute.
- Whisk in salt, sugar and melted butter.
- Slowly add flour, 1 cup at a time. Mix with a wooden spoon until the dough is smooth but still a bit sticky.
- Add more flour and knead until the dough is no longer sticky and is soft and smooth.
- Turn the dough out onto a lightly floured surface.
- Knead the dough for 3 minutes and shape into a ball. (*You can also use a stand mixer with dough attachment to make dough.*)

- Cover lightly with a towel and allow to rest for 10 minutes.
- Line 2 baking trays with silicone baking mats or baking paper. If using baking paper, lightly spray with cooking oil.
- Using a sharp knife, cut dough into ⅓ cup–sized pieces.
- Roll each piece of dough into a 50cm long rope. Take the ends and draw them together to form a circle on the benchtop.
- Twist the ends a couple of times, then bring them towards yourself and press them down gently onto the dough to make a pretzel shape. Place on prepared trays.
- Place bicarb soda and water in a large saucepan and bring to a boil.
- Drop 1 or 2 pretzels into the boiling water for 20 to 30 seconds only *(otherwise it may affect the flavour)*.
- Using a slotted spatula, lift the pretzels out of the water and allow excess water to drain off.
- Place pretzels onto the prepared baking trays. Sprinkle with sea salt. Repeat with remaining pretzels. *(If you want you can cover and refrigerate the boiled, unbaked pretzels for up to 24 hours before baking.)*
- Cook in oven at 200°C for 12 to 15 minutes or until golden brown.
- Remove from the oven and serve warm.

*Pretzels can be stored in an airtight container for up to 3 days.*

# Peanut Butter Bliss Balls

**Makes: 12 to 14**

*A healthy snack for brunch that the kids will love to help make. Try to use a natural peanut butter that doesn't have salt and sugar added.*

14 Medjool dates, pitted
200g raw or roasted almonds
⅓ cup peanut butter
1 tablespoon cacao powder
Crushed peanuts, to coat *(optional)*

**Method:**
• Line a baking tray with baking paper.
• Place pitted dates, almonds, peanut butter and cacao powder into a food processor. Process until mixture begins to form a ball and stick together. If the mixture looks and feels a bit dry, add an extra 1 to 2 tablespoons water. (*The mixture should feel a little sticky.*)
• Using your hands, roll a tablespoonful of the mixture into snack–size balls. Place on prepared tray.
• Place the crushed peanuts onto a plate and roll the balls in the nuts to coat.
• Return to the prepared tray and refrigerate for 30 minutes or until firm.
• Serve straight from the fridge or store them in an airtight container in the fridge for up to 5 days. Enjoy!

# Homemade Sausage Rolls

**Makes: 48**

*A recipe the kids can really get their hands into.*

2 small onions
3 cloves garlic
1 medium carrot
1 tablespoon milk
1 egg
500g veal or beef mince
500g sausage mince
¼ cup finely chopped parsley
2 tablespoons tomato sauce
¼ cup Worcestershire sauce
4 sheets ready rolled puff pastry, thawed

**Method:**

- Peel onions and garlic and finely chop. Peel and coarsely grate carrot.
- Peel and crush garlic.
- Line 2 large baking trays with baking paper.
- Whisk milk and egg together in a small jug.
- Place veal mince, sausage mince, onion, garlic, carrot, parsley, tomato and Worcestershire sauce in a large bowl. Season well.
- Lay a sheet of pastry on a chopping board. Cut sheet in half horizontally.
- Spoon ⅛ of the mince mixture down the long side of one pastry half, shaping mince into a long sausage shape. Brush opposite long edge with egg mixture.
- Roll up pastry to enclose filling, finishing seam side down.
- Cut roll into 6 small pieces. Place seam side down on the prepared tray, slightly apart. Brush tops with egg mixture.
- Repeat with remaining pastry, mince and egg mixture.
- Cook in oven at 200°C for 20 to 25 minutes or until golden brown and cooked through. Cool on a wire rack.

# Simple Scrolls

**Makes: 36**

*Get the kids in the kitchen to make these three different flavoured scrolls that are perfect for lunch boxes, after–school snacks or cheeky breakfasts.*

250g frozen spinach, thawed
40g pepperoni
50g sliced ham
225g can pineapple pieces
3 sheets ready rolled puff pastry, just thawed
150g ricotta
1 cup shredded tasty or pizza cheese
2 tablespoons pizza sauce

**Method:**
• Drain spinach well, squeezing out excess liquid.
• Slice pepperoni thinly. Chop ham into 2cm pieces.
• Drain pineapple pieces.
• Line two baking trays with baking paper.
• Place 1 pastry sheet on a chopping board.
• Spread with ricotta and top with spinach. Sprinkle over ⅓ of the cheese. Season well with salt and pepper.
• Starting from edge of the pastry, roll up to enclose the filling. Trim ends.
• Using a sharp knife, cut roll crossways into 12 slices. Place in a single layer on prepared tray.

- Place another pastry sheet on the chopping board.
- Spread with half the pizza sauce and top with the pepperoni. Sprinkle over half the remaining cheese.
- Roll up to enclose filling. Trim ends.
- Cut into 12 slices. Place in a single layer on tray.
- Place remaining pastry sheet on chopping board.
- Spread with remaining pizza sauce and top with ham and pineapple and remaining cheese.
- Roll up to enclose filling. Trim ends.
- Cut crossways into 12 slices. Place in a single layer on tray.
- Cook both trays in oven at 200°C for 25 minutes or until pastry is puffed and golden brown, swapping trays halfway through cooking.
- Remove from oven, cool on trays and serve warm or at room temperature.

# Apple & Banana Muffins
**Makes: 24**

*Use any apples you like in these muffins. Make sure they are a medium to large size so you get plenty of juicy apple in each muffin and make sure your bananas are really ripe.*

2 apples
2 cups plain flour
1 teaspoon bicarb soda
½ teaspoon ground nutmeg
½ teaspoon ground cinnamon
175g unsalted butter, softened
1¼ cups white sugar
1 teaspoon vanilla extract
2 eggs
¼ cup buttermilk
1 cup mashed bananas

**Method:**
• Peel, core and chop apples into 1 to 2cm pieces.
• Line 2 x 12 hole muffin pans with paper cases or baking paper squares.
• In a medium bowl sift together flour, bicarb soda, nutmeg and cinnamon.
• Beat butter, sugar and vanilla in large bowl of an electric mixer until light and creamy.
• Add eggs one at a time, beating well after each addition.
• Add flour mixture, buttermilk and banana, mix on a low speed until just combined. *(Don't overbeat or muffins will be tough.)*
• Remove bowl from mixer, using a spoon, fold in apples.

- Spoon mixture into prepared muffin pans filling each pan hole about halfway.
- Cook in oven at 190°C for 20 to 25 minutes or until a skewer or toothpick inserted in the centre comes out clean.

# Peanut Butter Porridge

**Serves: 2**

**CHEAP EATS**

*A perfect way to get started on a cold winter's morning.*

1 cup rolled oats *(not instant)*
2 tablespoons smooth peanut butter
2 tablespoons honey
2 teaspoons ground flaxseed
½ to 1 teaspoon ground cinnamon
1 peeled, grated apple *(optional)*

**Method:**
- Place 1 cup water and pinch of salt in a small saucepan, bring to a boil.
- Stir in oats, gently boil for 5 minutes or until thick and creamy, stirring occasionally. Remove from heat.
- Stir in peanut butter, honey, flaxseed, cinnamon and apple.
- Spoon into 2 bowls.

*Serve with your favourite milk or yoghurt.*

# Apple Crumble

**Serves: 4**

*This simple and delicious apple crumble is also perfect for a cold winter evening.*

4 medium apples
1 tablespoon lemon juice
1 tablespoon caster sugar

**CRUMBLE**
60g butter
⅓ cup plain flour
⅓ cup caster sugar
⅓ cup rolled oats

**Method:**
• Peel and core apples, chop into 2cm pieces.
• Place apples, lemon juice, sugar and ¼ cup water in a small saucepan over low to medium heat. Cover and cook, stirring for 3 minutes or until the apple is slightly softened.
• To make the crumble, chop butter into small pieces, place in a bowl with flour, sugar and oats.
• Using your fingertips, rub butter into flour mixture until mixture resembles coarse breadcrumbs.
• Place apple mixture into an ovenproof dish *(4 cup capacity)*. Sprinkle crumble mixture over apples.
• Cook in oven at 180°C for 20 to 25 minutes or until golden.

*Serve warm with ice cream or whipped cream.*

# Marmalade French Toast Sandwiches

**Serves: 6**

*An iconic family breakfast favourite, perfect for a lazy Sunday.*

250g tub cream cheese spread
12 slices sourdough bread
¾ cup orange marmalade
4 large eggs
2 tablespoons milk
Maple syrup *(optional)*

**Method:**
• Spread cream cheese over 6 slices of bread. Spread each one with marmalade. Top with remaining bread slices, pressing together to make sandwiches.
• Whisk eggs and milk together in a shallow bowl.
• Heat a lightly greased large frypan over a medium heat.
• Dip both sides of sandwiches into egg mixture. Place 2 or 3 sandwiches into the pan, cook 2 to 3 minutes each side or until golden brown. Repeat with remaining sandwiches.

*Serve drizzled with maple syrup.*

# Soups

The scent of bubbling soup packed with mouth–watering ingredients from meats and vegetables to spices and noodles will make any tummy grumble. All your favourites are here as well as something a bit different. Your midweek dinners just got easier – make a big batch at the beginning of the week and you'll have meals sorted for days.

# Chicken Noodle

**Serves: 4**

*No recipe book would be complete without a recipe for chicken noodle soup.*

2 large carrots
1 large onion
2 stalks celery
2 tablespoons olive oil
1 tablespoon minced garlic
2 bay leaves
2 litres chicken stock
500g chicken thigh fillets
180g thin egg noodles

**Method:**
• Peel carrots and onion. Chop into 1cm pieces.
• Chop celery into 1cm pieces.
• Heat oil in a stockpot over a medium heat. Add carrots, onions and celery, cook for 5 minutes, stirring occasionally.
• Add garlic and bay leaves, cook, stirring for 1 to 2 minutes.
• Pour in the stock, bring to a boil. Add chicken, cover partially with lid. Simmer for 20 to 25 minutes or until chicken is cooked and vegies are tender. Remove chicken from pot. Remove bay leaves and discard.
• Toss the noodles into pot, bring to a boil, cook for 4 to 5 minutes *(depending on the type of noodles used)* or until noodles are just cooked *(noodles will continue to cook as soup stands)*.
• While noodles are cooking, chop chicken into small pieces.
• Send the chicken back into the pot for a swim. Stir over a low heat until hot. Season with salt and pepper.

# Pea & Ham

**Serves: 4**

*This is traditional pea and ham soup at its best.*

1⅓ cups green split peas
2 carrots
1 large onion
3 cloves garlic
2 stalks celery
500g ham
2 tablespoons olive oil

**Method:**
• Rinse split peas well under running water. Drain.
• Peel carrots, onions and garlic and finely chop.
• Finely chop celery.
• Chop ham into 1 to 2cm pieces.

**TIP**
You can also use a smoked ham hock from the deli instead of the chopped ham. When soup is cooked, remove hock and chop or shred any meat into soup.

- Heat oil in a stockpot over a medium heat.
- Toss in the carrots, onion, garlic and celery.
- Cook, stirring, for 5 minutes or until vegies are slightly softened.
- Add split peas, ham and 1½ litres water. Bring to the boil over a high heat.
- Lower heat and simmer, covered, for 2 to 2½ hours or until split peas are very tender *(add extra water if soup gets too thick)*.

*Soak split peas overnight in cold water, so they cook more quickly.*

- Ladle out one third of the soup mixture into a heatproof bowl, cool slightly.
- Pour into a food processor bowl and process until smooth. Return to pot. Season to taste with salt and pepper.
- Cook over a low heat, stirring until soup is hot.

*Serve with buttered toast.*

# Broccoli

**Serves: 4**

*A beautiful soup for a cold day. Don't forget warm crusty bread for dipping!*

1kg broccoli
2 potatoes
1 large onion
2 cloves garlic
1 tablespoon butter
1 litre chicken stock
¾ cup cream or milk
1½ cups shredded cheddar cheese

**Method:**
• Trim broccoli stalks. Cut stalk and broccoli heads into small pieces.
• Peel potatoes and onion, chop into 2cm pieces.
• Peel and finely chop garlic.
• Melt butter in a stockpot over medium heat.
• Chuck in the onion and garlic, cook for 3 minutes or until onion is slightly softened.
• Pour in the stock, 1½ cups water, broccoli and potato. Bring to a boil.
• Lower heat, cover with lid and simmer 20 to 25 minutes or until broccoli and potatoes are cooked. Cool slightly.
• Using a stick mixer, blend until smooth. *(You can also do this in batches in a food processor.)*
• Return to a low heat, stirring until soup is hot.
• Turn off heat, stir in cream, then add cheese a handful at a time, stirring.
• Season with salt and freshly ground black pepper.

# Chicken & Sweet Corn

**Serves: 4**

*A Chinese–style soup perfect for any occasion. Drizzle with soy sauce and a little extra sesame oil if you like.*

2 spring onions
2 chicken breast fillets *(600g)*
1 litre chicken stock
1  tablespoon crushed ginger
2 chicken stock cubes
420g canned creamed corn
1 teaspoon sesame oil
1½ tablespoons cornflour
2 eggs

**Method:**
• Cut spring onions into thin slices.
• Place chicken in a stockpot with stock and 1 litre water. Cover with a lid, bring to a gentle boil, cook for about 15 to 20 minutes or until chicken is cooked, turning once.
• Remove chicken from pot, cool slightly, then slice or shred.
• Return stockpot to heat, add ginger, stock cubes, creamed corn, sesame oil, ¾ of the spring onions and sliced chicken. Bring to a boil.
• Mix cornflour with ¼ cup cold water until smooth. Gradually pour into soup, stirring until soup boils and thickens slightly.
• Beat eggs together with a large spoonful of the soup liquid, then drizzle into the pot slowly, gently stirring. Simmer 1 minute. Turn off heat.

*Serve soup sprinkled with remaining spring onions.*

# Curried Cauliflower & Coconut
**Serves: 4**

 *An Indian–inspired one–pot creamy curried cauliflower soup, with carrots, ginger and red lentils. Quick and easy to make.*

2 onions
1 medium cauliflower
½ cup red lentils
2 tablespoons olive oil
2 teaspoons minced ginger
2 teaspoons minced garlic
1 tablespoon curry powder
1 litre vegetable stock
¼ cup coconut cream

## Method:
• Peel and chop onions into 2cm pieces.
• Trim base and leaves from cauli, slice or chop cauli into small chunks.
• Rinse lentils in a sieve under running water, drain well.
• Heat oil in a stockpot over medium heat. Throw in the onions and cook for 3 to 4 minutes or until slightly softened.
• Toss in the ginger, garlic and curry powder, cook 1 to 2 minutes, stirring.
• Add in the cauli, lentils and stock. Bring to a boil. Lower heat, cover with lid and simmer for 20 to 25 minutes or until lentils and vegetables are very tender.
• Stir in coconut cream. Cool slightly.
• Using a stick mixer, blend soup until smooth. *(Add in extra water if soup is too thick.)*
• Return to low heat, stirring until soup is hot.

# Hearty Beef & Vegetable

**Serves: 4**

*This beef and vegie soup is like a meal in a bowl and it's filling!*

500g chuck steak or gravy beef
3 carrots
1 onion
2 potatoes
2 tablespoons olive oil
1 teaspoon minced garlic
2 tablespoons plain flour
1 litre beef stock
1½ cups dry red wine or beer
2 tablespoons tomato paste
1 teaspoon dried thyme leaves
1 cup frozen peas

## Method:
- Cut beef into 2cm pieces. Sprinkle with salt and pepper, toss.
- Peel carrots and onion, chop into 1cm pieces.
- Peel and chop potatoes into 2cm pieces.
- Heat oil in a stockpot over a high heat. Add beef in two batches, cook until browned. *(Add a little extra oil if needed.)* Remove beef.
- Toss in the onion, carrot and garlic, cook stirring for 3 minutes or until onion is slightly softened.
- Stir in flour, cook for 1 minute. Gradually stir in stock.
- Pour in wine or beer, 2 cups water, tomato paste, thyme and beef. Cover with lid, bring to a boil. Lower heat and simmer for 1¼ hours or until beef is almost tender.
- Chuck in the potatoes and peas, simmer covered for a further 20 to 25 minutes or until potatoes are cooked and beef is very tender.

*Serve with crusty bread rolls or with hot buttered toast.*

# Thai Carrot & Sweet Potato

**Serves: 4**

*Serve this nutritious, Thai spiced soup with chopped fresh coriander and a good squeeze of fresh lime juice.*

2 medium *(1kg)* sweet potatoes
2 onions
3 large carrots
1 tablespoon oil
1 teaspoon minced garlic
1 tablespoon minced ginger
2 tablespoons red curry paste
1 litre vegetable stock
¼ cup peanut butter

**Method:**
• Peel sweet potatoes and onions. Chop into 2 to 3cm pieces.
• Peel and slice carrots.
• Heat oil in a stockpot over a medium heat.
• Throw in onions, garlic and ginger, cook for 3 to 4 minutes or until onions are slightly softened.
• Stir in curry paste, cook for 1 to 2 minutes or until paste is bubbling.
• In a small bowl, whisk together ½ cup hot water with the peanut butter until smooth.
• Add to the pot with carrots, sweet potatoes and stock, stir well.
• Cover with lid and boil gently for 20 to 25 minutes or until the vegies are well cooked. Remove from heat and cool slightly.
• Using a stick mixer, blend soup until smooth. *(You can also do this in batches in a food processor.)*
• Return to pot, stir over a low heat until hot. Season with salt.

# 5-Ingredient Dumpling

**Serves: 4**

*Use your favourite frozen dumplings. In winter I like to keep a large bag of dumplings in the freezer, ready to make an easy, warm–you–up meal. Add more tom yum or laksa paste if you like it spicy.*

1 bunch baby bok choy
200g button mushrooms
1½ litres chicken stock
¼ cup tom yum or laksa paste
400g frozen dumplings

**Method:**
• Wash bok choy well. Trim base and cut leaves and stem into thick slices.
• Cut mushrooms into quarters.
• Add stock and paste into a stockpot. Bring to the boil.
• Add dumplings and gently boil for 5 minutes.
• Add bok choy and mushrooms and gently boil for another 5 minutes or until dumplings are cooked.

# Minestrone
**Serves: 4**

*Serve this warm and filling soup with some fresh buttered crusty bread rolls to create a winter's meal. I like mine with parmesan on top.*

2 stalks celery
3 rindless bacon rashers
2 carrots
1 potato
2 cloves garlic
400g can red kidney beans
2 tablespoons olive oil
1 litre beef stock
400g can chopped tomatoes
1 cup small shell pasta

**Method:**
• Chop celery and bacon into 1cm pieces.
• Peel carrots and potato. Chop into 2cm pieces.
• Peel and finely chop garlic.
• Rinse and drain kidney beans.
• Place the oil, celery, bacon, carrots, potato and garlic in a stockpot and stir to combine. Cook over medium heat, for 5 minutes, or until vegies are slightly softened.
• Add the stock and tomatoes to pot, bring to a boil.
• Lower heat, simmer, covered for 25 to 30 minutes or until vegetables are almost cooked.
• Chuck in the pasta and kidney beans, gently boil uncovered for 8 to 10 minutes or until pasta is just cooked. Season with salt and pepper.

# Curried Lentil & Vegetable

**Serves: 4**

*A quick, healthy and delicious vegetarian soup using budget–friendly ingredients. Instead of a soup pack, you can use your favourite combo of any of these vegies: carrot, onion, parsnip, potato, celery, swede.*

1 pkt *(1kg)* soup vegetables
1 cup red lentils
2 tablespoons olive oil
2 teaspoons minced garlic
2 teaspoons crushed ginger
1 tablespoon curry powder
½ teaspoon fennel seeds
2 teaspoons cumin seeds
2 litres salt-reduced vegetable stock

**Method:**
• Peel and wash vegies. Chop into 1cm pieces.
• Rinse lentils in a sieve under running water, drain well.
• Heat oil in a stockpot over medium heat. Throw in the garlic, ginger and vegies and cook, stirring for 4 minutes or until slightly softened.
• Chuck in the curry powder, fennel and cumin seeds. Cook for 2 minutes or until spices smell roasted.
• Stir in lentils, stock and 1 cup of water, bring to a boil. Lower heat, gently boil uncovered for 30 minutes or until vegetables are tender. Add in extra water if soup becomes too thick.
• Season with salt and pepper.

*Serve with chopped parsley or coriander and a wedge of lemon.*

# Pumpkin

**Serves: 4 to 6**

*This is a classic, easy pumpkin soup made with fresh pumpkin. It's very easy to make, thick, creamy and full of flavour.*

1.2kg pumpkin

1 large onion

2 cloves garlic

1 litre chicken or vegetable stock

½ cup cream

*Butternut pumpkin is my favourite in this soup.*

## Method:

- Cut skin and scoop out seeds from pumpkin. Cut into 3 to 4cm chunks.
- Peel onion and garlic and roughly chop.
- Place pumpkin, onion, garlic and stock in a stockpot *(liquid won't quite cover all the pumpkin).*
- Bring to a boil, lower heat, cover with a lid and gently boil until pumpkin is very tender *(check with butter knife),* about 20 to 25 minutes. Remove from heat, cool slightly.
- Use a stick mixer to blend until smooth. *(You can also do this in a food processor in batches.)*
- Return to low heat, stirring until soup is hot.
- Season to taste with salt and pepper, stir through cream.

*Serve with crusty bread rolls.*

# Cheat's Chicken Pho

**Serves: 4**

*This is an easy version of a popular Vietnamese soup. Use any thickness of rice noodle you like.*

700g chicken thigh fillets
250g dried rice noodles
2 tablespoons oil
2 teaspoons minced garlic
1 tablespoon crushed ginger
2 litres chicken stock
¼ cup hoisin sauce
1 tablespoon fish sauce

**Method:**
- Cut chicken into slices.
- Cook noodles according to packet directions, drain and rinse under cold water. Drain well.
- Heat oil in a stockpot over a medium heat. Add chicken and cook until starting to turn golden.
- Add in the garlic and ginger, cook stirring 1 to 2 minutes or until garlic and ginger start to change colour.
- Pour in the stock, hoisin sauce and fish sauce. Bring to a boil, lower heat, cover with a lid and simmer for 15 minutes. Season to taste with extra hoisin sauce, fish sauce and ground black pepper.
- Place rice noodles into bowls and ladle over hot soup.

*Serve soup topped with any of the following: sliced white onion, fresh bean sprouts, coriander sprigs, sliced red chilli, lemon wedges.*

# Quick Tomato
**Serves: 4**

1 large onion
400g can cooked lentils
2 tablespoons olive oil
2 x 400g cans chopped tomatoes
1 litre vegetable stock
1 cup fresh basil leaves
½ cup grated parmesan cheese

**Method:**
- Peel and chop onion into 1 to 2cm pieces.
- Drain and rinse lentils.
- Heat oil in a stockpot over a medium heat. Toss in the onion and cook stirring for 5 minutes or until softened.
- Chuck in the tomatoes, stock, lentils and most of the basil leaves. (*Leave a few for the top of soup.*) Bring to a boil, lower heat and simmer for 25 to 30 minutes or until slightly thickened. Remove from heat, cool slightly.
- Using a stick mixer blend soup until almost smooth.
- Stir over a low heat until hot.
- Season with salt and pepper.
- Serve with remaining basil leaves and parmesan.

*It's nice for the soup to still have a bit of texture.*

# Italian Meatball
**Serves: 4**

1 large onion
2 zucchini
1 tablespoon olive oil
400g pkt fresh pork and veal meatballs
180g pkt McKenzie's minestrone soup kit
2 x 400g can chopped tomatoes
200g tub of fresh basil pesto *(optional)*

**Method:**
- Peel and chop onion finely. Chop zucchini into 2cm pieces.
- Heat oil in a stockpot over a medium heat. Throw in the meatballs and cook until browned. Remove from pot.
- Add in the onion to stockpot and cook stirring for 3 to 4 minutes or until softened.
- Pour in 2 litres boiling water, minestrone mix, stock sachet and tomatoes. Bring to a boil.
- Lower heat, cover with a lid and simmer for 30 minutes. Add meatballs and zucchini, simmer covered for 20 minutes or until meatballs and soup mix are cooked.
- Season with salt and pepper.
- Serve with a spoonful of pesto in each bowl.

**TIP**

If you can't find this dried soup kit in the supermarket, use another type of dried soup mix and 2 stock cubes instead.

# Indigenous Favourites

Our culture might be over 60,000 years old – the oldest living culture in the world – but over the last 50 to 60 years, we have developed a "modern" Indigenous culture. Here are just a few recipes from this as well as a few from overseas.

# Bully Beef & Rice
**Serves: 4**

*This dish is a family favourite and has fed many a hungry Koori kid. With tins of corned beef being popular to many peoples of the Pacific, Bully Beef & Rice has been adopted by Indigenous people from all over Australia. Another dish reminiscent of the days of when fresh meat was inaccessible to Aboriginal and Torres Strait Islander people.*

3 potatoes
2 carrots
1 large onion
2 cloves garlic
2 tablespoons oil
340g can corned beef
2 cups chopped cabbage
2 tablespoons soy sauce

## Method:
• Peel potatoes, carrots, onion and garlic. Chop into 1cm pieces.
• Heat oil in a large frypan over a medium heat. Cook onion for 5 minutes or until softened. Stir in garlic, cook for 1 minute.
• Add contents of canned corned beef into frying pan and cook stirring until all the meat, onions and garlic are well mixed.
• Throw in your diced potatoes and carrots and add enough water to almost cover the vegetables. Boil gently for 10 to 15 minutes, or until potatoes are nice and soft. While ya wait, listen to some Charlie Pride.
• Lastly chuck in your diced cabbage. Cook for another 5 minutes or until cabbage is tender. Season well with salt and pepper.

*Serve generously on a warm bed of freshly cooked rice. Have some madfeedz.*

# Curried Sausages
**Serves: 4 to 6 people**

*A Koori family classic that's been cooked for generations. A flexible meal that lets you add and remove different vegies to suit yourself.*

1 large onion
2 apples
¼ cup vegetable oil
8 beef sausages
1 tablespoon Keen's curry powder
1 tablespoon plain flour
2 cups chicken stock
¼ cup raisins
1 cup sliced green beans
2 tablespoons cream

**Method:**
- Peel onion and slice.
- Peel, core and cut each apple into 8 wedges.
- Heat 2 tablespoons of the oil in ya big old favourite saucepan over medium heat.
- Chuck the sausages in and brown all over, remove and set aside.
- Add the remaining oil to pan and cook onion stirring for 3 minutes or until slightly softened.
- Stir in curry powder and flour, mix well. Slowly pour in stock, stirring until sauce boils and thickens.
- Toss apples, raisins and sausages into pan and bring to the boil. Lower heat and simmer for 15 to 20 minutes.
- Stir in beans and cream, cook for 5 minutes. Season to taste with salt and black pepper.

*Enjoy them keenaz madfeedz!*

# Johnny Cakes

**Serves: 4 to 6**

*A quick traditional favourite, fantastic with soups or curries or served with condiments.*

1 cup plain flour
1 cup self raising flour
Pinch of salt
1 teaspoon extra virgin olive oil
¾ cup milk or water
Vegetable oil, for frying

**Method:**

• Mix flours and salt together in a bowl.
• Add oil, milk or water, stirring then kneading until a soft dough is formed.
• Break off pieces of dough *(slightly smaller than a tennis ball)* and flatten with your hand on a lightly floured benchtop.
• Heat a thin layer of oil in a frypan over medium heat or grease a barbecue plate with oil. Cook Johnny cakes for about 4 to 5 minutes each side or until golden brown.

*Traditionally, these were cooked on the hot coals removed from a fire.*

# Damper

**Serves: 4**

 *A traditional bush bread originally made from native plants, it's fantastic with soups or made into sandwiches.*

3 cups self raising flour
¼ teaspoon salt
90g chilled butter
¾ cup water

**Method:**

• Preheat oven to 200°C. Line a baking tray with baking paper.
• Cut butter into 1cm pieces.
• Mix together flour and salt in a large bowl. Get in there and use your fingertips to rub butter pieces into flour until mixture resembles fine breadcrumbs.
• Gradually add the water into flour mixture, using a butter knife to stir until mixture just comes together. Add an extra 1 to 2 tablespoons water if the mixture is a little dry, like the Broncos defence. Use your hands to bring the mixture together into a dough.
• Place dough on a lightly floured benchtop and knead gently until smooth (*don't overknead*). Place on prepared tray and shape into an 18cm round and flatten slightly.
• Use a sharp knife dipped in flour to cut slightly into dough and mark 8 wedges on top.
• Dust the damper with a little extra flour. Cook in oven for 30 minutes or until damper is cooked through and sounds lubly and hollow when tapped on the base. Transfer to a wire rack to cool slightly.

*Serve warm or at room temperature with butter or whatever you want.*

# Curried Eggs

**Serves: 4**

*A party favourite for decades, this classic is great fresh or on a sandwich.*

6 large eggs
1 stalk celery
¼ cup mayonnaise
1 tablespoon Dijon mustard
1¼ teaspoons curry powder
¼ teaspoon salt
¼ teaspoon black pepper

TIP

I love using Kewpie mayo in this. You can also use reduced fat mayo.

## Method:

- Place eggs in the bottom of a large saucepan and cover with cold water.
- Bring to a boil over high heat. Boil 1 minute. Turn off heat.
- Cover pan with lid and let them eggs sit for 20 minutes.
- Meanwhile, chop celery into 1cm pieces. *(You will need about ¼ cup.)*
- After 20 minutes, drain eggs and rinse well with cold water. Peel eggs and place in refrigerator for at least 30 minutes to cool.
- Finely chop them eggs up, like Souths chopped Canterbury in 2014, and place in a bowl.
- Add celery, mayonnaise, mustard, curry powder, salt and pepper *(You can add another tablespoon of mayonnaise if you want it a little creamier.)*

*Spoon into crisp lettuce leaves, roll up and eat!*

# Chicken Rolls

**Serves: 4**

*One of those meals that's cheap and easy when you've had a long day.*

1 large cooked roast *(barbecued)* chicken
8 soft dinner rolls
Butter, to spread
1 large container of pasta or potato salad

**Method:**
• Remove meat from chicken and shred.
• Split rolls in half and butter the inside of the rolls.
• Fill with chicken then salad.
• Close rolls and enjoy the quick, easy dinner!

*Normally, I just poke a hole into side of bun to make a pocket-style bun that's easy to eat, especially for the kids!*

# Koori Noodles

**Serves: 1 to 2**

*A quick, cheap and easy meal that's perfect for any time of the day.*

72g pkt *(2 minute)* instant noodles
1 teaspoon curry powder
1 teaspoon minced garlic
¾ cup grated devon
1 egg
½ cup shredded cheese

## Method:

- Add 2 cups water to a medium saucepan. Bring to a boil.
- Add noodles, noodle seasoning, curry powder, garlic and grated devon. Gently boil for 2 minutes or until noodles are almost cooked.
- Add egg and stir through with a fork, boil for 1 minute. Drain off excess liquid.

*Served topped with cheese.*

# Chilli Beef Noodles

**Serves: 1 to 2**

*I put this together in a hurry one night using what I had in the pantry and it was delicious!*

72g pkt *(2 minute)* instant noodles
250g piece of steak
Chilli—infused oil
1 tablespoon vegetable oil
1 egg

**Method:**
- Add 1 litre water to a medium saucepan. Bring to a boil.
- Add noodles and boil for 2 minutes or until cooked. Remove noodles and drain, leaving cooking liquid in saucepan.
- Meanwhile, season steak with salt and chilli oil.
- Heat vegetable oil in frypan over medium to high heat. Add steak, cook until browned on both sides and cooked as you like it. Remove from pan.
- Return saucepan with cooking liquid to a high heat and bring to a boil.
- Lower heat, crack egg into saucepan and simmer for 2 minutes or until egg is cooked to your liking. Remove egg, set aside. Drain liquid from saucepan.
- To serve, slice steak into bite—size pieces, add to saucepan with noodles, noodle seasoning and 1 tablespoon of chilli oil. Mix well.
- Place noodles and beef on a plate and top with egg.

*Use your favourite steak here and any flavour noodles you like.*

# 'Egg on Top' Chicken Noodles

**Serves: 1 to 2**

*This was one of the meals I threw together one lunchtime using leftover chicken from last night's dinner and a packet of noodles, and it was deadly as.*

85g pkt Mi Goreng instant noodles
250g shredded cooked chicken breast
1 egg

## Method:

- Add 1 litre water to a medium saucepan. Bring to a boil.
- Add noodles and boil for 2 minutes or until cooked. Remove noodles and drain, leaving cooking liquid in saucepan. Place noodles in a bowl.
- Add seasoning from packet and shredded chicken to noodles, mix well.
- Return saucepan with cooking liquid to a high heat and bring to a boil.
- Lower heat, crack egg into saucepan and simmer for 2 minutes or until cooked to your liking.
- Remove egg, place on top of noodles and serve.

*Drizzle over some soy sauce if you like.*

# Dough Boys
**Makes: 6**

*These are to add to the NZ-Style Boil Up recipe (page 83) or for any other stew or soup. They are like a dumpling – some people don't like 'em, but me I love them.*

1 cup plain flour
1 teaspoon baking powder
Cold water

**Method:**
• Mix together flour and baking powder in a bowl.
• Gradually add water a small amount at a time, stirring with a butter knife to make a soft, smooth dough.
• Shape into 6 small balls. *(They double in size when cooked.)*
• Add to pot of simmering soup or stew about 5 to 10 minutes before serving, turning occasionally while cooking.

# NZ-Style Boil Up

**Serves: 6**

*Kia Ora! Another childhood fave! This one is from my friend's nanna's house in NZ.*

4–8 *(1¼kg)* pork or lamb bone pieces
6 thick sausages
2 large bunches of watercress
¼ cabbage
4 large potatoes
1 large sweet potato
3 carrots
1 large onion
6 dough boys *(see recipe page 82)*

## Method:

- Place bones and sausages in a large stockpot. Cover well with water.
- Bring to a boil, then lower heat and simmer until meat on bones is tender and is almost falling off the bone. *(Top up with water if level drops below meat.)*
- Wash watercress well. Roughly chop watercress and cabbage.
- Peel potatoes, sweet potato and carrots and chop into 2 to 3cm pieces. Peel and slice onion.
- Skim fat and any skum from top of pot and discard. Remove bones and shred away any meat, add meat back into pot and discard bones.
- Add all vegetables including watercress to pot and gently boil for about 20 to 25 minutes or until vegetables are just cooked. Season well with salt and pepper.
- Meanwhile, make dough boys and add to the pot when vegies are cooked. Simmer for 5 to 10 minutes, stirring occasionally until cooked in the centre.

*Served traditionally with lots of buttered bread.*

# Fry Bread

**Serves: 8**

 *A Maori friend of mine put me onto this recipe and it's been a favourite in my house since. Normally, these fried breads are served with jam or something sweet, but they also go well with the curries and other savoury meals in this book.*

3½ cups self raising flour
½ teaspoon salt
Cold water
Vegetable oil, for deep frying

**Method:**
• Place flour and salt in a large bowl.
• Gradually add enough cold water to make a soft dough, mix with a Bronco's wooden spoon, but don't overmix!
• Let dough rest for 30 minutes in bowl, covered with a tea towel.
• Place dough on a lightly floured benchtop and press or roll dough out to 1½cm thickness.
• Cut into 6cm x 6cm squares or whatever shape you like.
• Heat oil in a large saucepan. Deep fry in batches of 2 or 3 pieces until golden brown on both sides. Remove from oil and drain on paper towel.

TIP

If you overmix, this will cause bread to become tough and flat.

# Crocodile Steak

**Serves: 1 to 2**

*Watch this crocodile rock around ya frypan as you grill up some deadly meals. Croc is available from selected supermarkets.*

250g piece crocodile steak
Steak spice *(or salt and black pepper)*
1 tablespoon olive oil

## Method

- If crocodile is frozen, thaw in the refrigerator overnight.
- Wipe away the moisture off the surface of crocodile steak with paper towel. If cooking for two, cut in half.
- Rub croc steak with olive oil and sprinkle all over with steak spice *(or salt and black pepper).*
- Heat a frypan over a low to medium heat, add the croc steak and cook for about 4 to 5 minutes, covered with a lid until golden brown on base.
- Flip over to brown the other side and continue cooking uncovered until croc is cooked through.

*Serve him up with your favourite side like mash or salad.*

# Chikalicious

Chicken is king when it comes to cooking, being so versatile and able to be used in so many fantastic ways. Whether it's in a schnitzel, sliced, diced, stuffed ... it's an amazing bird to work with. In this section, you'll see just a few ways I use this delicious meat and how it can be enjoyed by the family.

# Koori Curry Chicken

**Serves: 2 to 3**

*The ultimate Koori classic, a traditional meal had for generations.*

500g chicken breast fillets
2 large potatoes
1 large carrot
1 large onion
2 tablespoons oil
400ml can coconut cream
1 to 2 tablespoons curry powder

## Method:

• Cut chicken into 2cm pieces.
• Peel and slice potatoes and carrot. Peel and chop onion.
• Heat oil in a large frypan or saucepan. Throw in the chicken and onion and fry up until chicken is lightly browned.
• Stir in coconut cream and curry powder and bring to a boil.
• Gently throw in potatoes and carrot, cover with a lid and simmer until vegetables and chicken are cooked. Season with salt and pepper.

*Serve with rice.*

*For a quicker meal you can add the carrots and potatoes in at the same time.*

# One Pan Chicken Dinner

**Serves: 4**

*A quick and easy meal that'll be a winner winner chicken dinner in your household.*

1 tablespoon oil
500g chicken mince
420g can of peas, corn and carrots
500g pasta *(I normally use small shells)*
1 litre chicken stock

**Method:**
- Heat oil in a large frypan or saucepan and fry up chicken mince until cooked and lightly browned.
- Drain peas, corn and carrot, add to pan with pasta.
- Pour over chicken stock, mix well and bring to a boil.
- Lower heat and gently boil until pasta is cooked and stock is reduced. *(Add a little extra water if needed.)*
- Season with salt and pepper.

I like to have it straight on hot toast.

# Chicken Sausage Curry
**Serves: 4**

*A delicious go–to meal that will win them over every time.*

2 large potatoes
1 large carrot
1 large onion
1 tablespoon oil
600g pkt chicken sausages
400ml can coconut cream
1 to 2 tablespoons curry powder

**Method:**
• Peel and slice potatoes and carrot.
• Peel onion, chop into 1cm pieces.
• Heat oil in a large frypan over a medium heat. Chuck your
  chicken sausages and onion in the pan and fry up until onion is
  lightly browned and sausages are cooked enough to cut.
• Remove from heat. Remove sausages and cut into bite–
  size pieces.
• Return pan to heat, throw in potatoes, carrot, onion, sausages,
  coconut cream and curry powder.
• Simmer until vegetables and sausages are cooked. Season with
  salt and pepper.

*Serve with rice.*

# Garlic & Herb Roast Chicken

**Serves: 4 to 6**

*A classic roast chicken that the mob will love.*

1 large fresh chicken *(1.5–2kg)*
1 head of garlic
1 lemon
2 tablespoons chopped parsley
2 tablespoons olive oil
1 tablespoon melted butter
2 tablespoons dry white wine *(optional)*
3 or 4 fresh rosemary sprigs

**Method:**
- Crank that oven up to 190°C.
- Pat chicken dry with paper towel. Place in a greased baking dish.
- Remove 2 to 3 cloves of garlic from bulb and crush. Leave remaining bulb for stuffing chicken.
- Squeeze one half of lemon, just enough for one tablespoon of juice. Set lemon halves aside.
- Mix together lemon juice, parsley, olive oil, melted butter and wine *(if using)*. Pour all over the chicken rubbing in under the skin and inside the cavity.
- Season chicken well inside and outside with salt and pepper.
- Rub the crushed garlic all over the chicken and under the skin.
- Stuff the remaining bulb of garlic into the chicken cavity along with the rosemary sprigs and the squeezed lemon half. *(You can also use thyme, sage or tarragon.)*

*I do this separately as one of the last steps to maximise the garlic taste.*

- Cook chicken in preheated oven, basting with pan juices once or twice during cooking. Cooking time will depend on the size of your chicken – allow about 25 minutes per 500g. A 2kg chicken will take approx 1 hour 40 to 1 hour 50 minutes to cook. To check chicken is cooked, insert a knife between the breast and leg – the juices should run clear, not pink! Remove chicken from oven and rest for 10 minutes to keep all of those juices in before slicing.

# Chicken Curry Noodles

**Serves: 1**

*A delightful quick, easy snack or one for the tucker box.*

72g pkt chicken flavoured instant noodles
1 tablespoon oil
250g diced or minced chicken
1 teaspoon curry powder
1 egg

**Method:**
- Cook noodles according to packet directions. Drain well.
- Heat oil in a frypan. Add chicken and fry up until golden brown and cooked.
- Stir in noodles and curry powder, return to a medium heat.
- Pour over lightly beaten egg, stirring until well combined with noodles and cooked through.

**TIP**
Adjust amount of curry powder to suit your taste.

*Serve with some soy or chilli sauce.*

# Chicken Schnitzel

**Makes: 8**

*A basic recipe that'll open the door to so many amazing meals.*

4 chicken breast fillets
3 eggs
1 cup plain flour
2½ cups dried breadcrumbs
Vegetable oil, for deep frying

**Method:**
- Slice each breast fillet horizontally in half to make 2 thinner pieces. Use a meat mallet to flatten each piece into a thinner schnitzel shape.
- Beat eggs well with a fork.
- Place beaten eggs, flour and breadcrumbs into separate bowls.
- Coat each piece of chicken in flour and shake off excess.
- Dip in the egg mixture until well–coated all over, drain off excess egg.
- Coat in the breadcrumbs pressing on firmly. Place on a tray, layering with a sheet of plastic wrap or baking paper so they don't stick together. Refrigerate until ready to cook.
- Heat oil in a large deep saucepan or a deep fryer. Cook in batches over a medium heat until golden brown and chicken is cooked through. Drain on paper towel.

*Enjoy with your favourite sides, sauces, or on a sandwich or schnitty roll.*

# Green Chicken Curry

**Serves: 2 to 3**

*Definitely a favourite of mine, originally from Thailand. Love adding fresh chopped chilli to spice it up.*

500g chicken thigh fillets
1 onion
100g green beans
1 zucchini
1 tablespoon oil
¼ cup green curry paste
1 cup chicken stock
400ml can coconut milk
1 tablespoon fish sauce
¼ cup fresh coriander leaves

**Method:**
- Cut chicken into thin slices.
- Peel onion, halve and slice.
- Trim beans and cut in half. Trim zucchini and cut into 1cm thick slices.
- Heat oil in a large saucepan over high heat. Chuck in the chicken and onion and fry up for 3 to 4 minutes or until onion is softened.
- Stir in curry paste and cook for 1 minute or until fragrant.
- Stir in stock and coconut milk.
- Bring to a boil. Lower heat and simmer, covered for 10 minutes.
- Stir in green beans, zucchini and fish sauce. Simmer, uncovered for a further 3 to 4 minutes or until beans are tender.
- Remove from heat. Stir through coriander leaves.

*Serve with freshly cooked jasmine rice.*

# Spinach & Ricotta Baked Chicken

**Serves: 1**

*This is one I made up for the wife – one of her favourite meals.*

100g baby spinach leaves
1 large chicken breast
1 slice ham
250g ricotta
1 tablespoon honey
1 teaspoon minced garlic

## Method:

- Place spinach and a little water into a saucepan, cover with a lid and bring to a boil. Cook until spinach is wilted.
- Remove from pan and drain well, cool slightly and squeeze out excess liquid.
- Slice chicken breast almost in half through the side to make a large pocket.
- Place ham slice into pocket, folding ham over.
- Mix together spinach and ricotta and place inside the ham fold.
- Close breast pocket firmly and place onto a large piece of foil.
- Drizzle honey over chicken, spread over garlic and wrap chicken in foil. Place on an oven tray.
- Cook in oven at 220°C for about 20 to 25 minutes or until chicken juices run clear in colour when pierced with a knife in the centre.

> *I normally serve this with a whole roasted sweet potato with honey butter, as that's her favourite side.*

# Slow Cooker Cheesy Chicken & Rice

**Serves: 4 to 6**

*A perfect meal for a cold day.*

1 large onion
2 chicken breast fillets
420g can cream of chicken soup
400g can creamed corn
2 cups white rice
2 litres chicken stock
2 cups shredded tasty cheese

## Method:
- Peel onion, chop finely.
- Place chicken in base of the slow cooker bowl.
- Sprinkle over chopped onion.
- Pour over chicken soup and creamed corn.
- Sprinkle over rice. *(I like medium grain white rice for this, but you can use whatever you have.)*
- Pour stock gently over rice.
- Cover and cook on Low for 7 to 8 hours or on High for 3½ to 4 hours.
- A few minutes before serving, remove chicken and shred with a fork.
- Return shredded chicken to the slow cooker with cheese and stir through.

*Serve sprinkled with lots of fresh chopped parsley.*

# Chicken, Bacon & Mushroom Pasta

**Serves: 4**

*Leave the mushrooms out if the kids aren't keen!*

400g penne pasta
500g chicken thigh fillets
200g bacon
2 teaspoons minced garlic
200g button mushrooms
2 tablespoons oil
1 large chicken stock cube
300ml carton cream

## Method:
• Cook pasta in a large saucepan of boiling, salted water until just cooked. Drain and return to saucepan, set aside.
• Meanwhile, cut chicken into 2cm pieces.
• Trim fat from bacon and chop into 1cm pieces.
• Slice mushrooms.
• Heat oil in a large frypan over a high heat. Chuck in chicken and fry that up until chicken changes colour, about 5 minutes.
• Add bacon and garlic and cook for another 5 minutes or until golden brown.
• Stir in mushrooms, stock cube, cream and ¼ cup water. Boil gently for 4 to 5 minutes or until the sauce thickens slightly. Season with black pepper.
• Stir sauce into pasta in saucepan, heat until pasta is hot and well–coated in sauce. *(Add a little water if sauce is too thick.)*

*Serve with grated parmesan.*

# Chicken Rice Bowl

**Serves: 4**

*Make this up for lunch one day and take to work the next!*

450g pkt microwave brown rice
500g chicken tenderloins
2 tablespoons Moroccan spice
3 tablespoons olive oil
150g feta cheese
100g rocket leaves
½ cup dried currants
⅓ cup toasted pine nuts
2 lemons

## Method:
- Heat rice according to packet directions, place on a plate and throw into the fridge until cold.
- Meanwhile, coat chicken in spice mix.
- Heat 2 tablespoons of the oil in a large frypan over high heat. Fry chicken in two batches until cooked through, about 3 minutes each side. Remove from heat and cut chicken into thick slices. Cool slightly.
- Crumble feta into a serving bowl.
- Add rocket, currants, rice, chicken and pine nuts.
- Finely grate half of 1 lemon over the salad, then squeeze over juice from both lemons.
- Drizzle over remaining 1 tablespoon of olive oil and season with salt and pepper. Toss ingredients together.

# Easy Chicken Enchiladas

**Serves: 4**

*Choose whether you want mild or spicy salsa.*

1 large barbecue chicken
12 *(312g pkt)* white corn or wheat tortillas
2 cups Mexican-style grated cheese
½ x 400g can black beans
2 x 300g jars tomato salsa dip

**Method:**
• Remove meat from chicken, shred into small pieces, discarding
  bones and skin.
• Heat tortillas according to packet directions.
• Divide chicken evenly along the centre of tortillas and sprinkle
  each one with 1 tablespoon of cheese.
• Roll up to enclose and place seam side down in a large, greased
  ovenproof dish.
• Rinse and drain black beans and add to salsa.
• Spoon salsa mixture over tortillas, sprinkle with remaining
  cheese.
• Cook in oven at 200°C for 20 minutes or until the cheese is
  melted and chicken is heated through.

*Serve with salad and sliced avocado or a dollop of guacamole dip.*

# Sticky Spicy Chicken Wings

**Serves: 4**

 *You won't be able to stop eating these –*
*a weeknight hero!*

1¼kg chicken wings
1 teaspoon garlic powder
1 teaspoon onion powder
⅓ cup hoisin sauce
¼ cup soy sauce
1 tablespoon sriracha sauce

## Method:

- Place chicken wings in a large plastic bag and toss together with the garlic and onion powder.
- Line base of a large baking dish with baking paper. Place wings in dish.
- Cook in oven at 200°C for 30 minutes or until golden. Remove from oven.
- Mix together sauces and ⅓ cup water and pour over wings, turning wings in the sauce.
- Return to oven for a further 20 minutes or until wings are cooked and sauce is glazed and sticky. *(Add a little extra water if sauce gets too thick.)*

*Serve with rice or as they are.*

# Yum Yum Chicken

**Serves: 3 to 4**

 *You can use other cuts of chicken in this. Thigh fillets and wing pieces work well, just adjust the cooking time to suit, adding a little water if needed.*

⅓ cup soy sauce
⅓ cup shao hsing or dry sherry
2 tablespoons brown sugar
750g chicken drumstick fillets
½ bunch spring onions
2 tablespoons sesame oil
1 tablespoon minced garlic
1 tablespoon crushed ginger

**Method:**
- Mix soy sauce, shao hsing and brown sugar together. Add chicken and toss to coat.
- Cut spring onions into 4cm lengths.
- Heat sesame oil over a low heat in a large heavy base saucepan or pot.
- Chuck in the garlic and ginger and cook stirring until golden.
- Toss in the chicken with marinade and the white section of spring onions. *(Leave the green tops for later.)*
- Bring to a boil, lower heat, cover with lid and simmer for 15 minutes.
- Remove lid, stir and simmer another 5 to 10 minutes or until chicken is cooked and tender and the sauce is thickened and syrupy. *(Add extra water if sauce starts to stick.)*
- Stir through green spring onion tops.

*Serve with steamed rice.*

# Crispy Fried Chicken

**Serves: 4**

*Soaking the chicken in buttermilk makes it tender and juicy when it's cooked.*

8 to 10 chicken drumsticks
1½ cups buttermilk
1¼ cups plain flour
1 tablespoon smoked paprika
3 teaspoons onion powder
3 teaspoons garlic powder
2 teaspoons salt
Vegetable oil, for deep frying

**Method:**

- Place chicken and buttermilk in a large bowl and toss to coat. Cover and refrigerate for a few hours or overnight.
- In a bowl, mix together flour, paprika, onion and garlic powder and salt.
- Coat chicken drumsticks in flour mixture one at a time, shaking off any excess.
- Heat oil in a large deep frypan or deep fryer over medium heat. Cook chicken in 2 to 3 batches until golden brown all over, about 4 to 5 minutes.
- Place chicken on a greased wire rack sitting over a baking dish. Cook in the oven at 200°C for about 20 to 25 minutes or until chicken is cooked through.

TIP

Eat these crunchy drumsticks with coleslaw and mashed potato for a meal or dip in your favourite sauce and eat as they are.

# Roo

Australia's first fast food, kangaroo is a lean meat with less than 2 per cent fat, making it a healthier red meat option. It's in most supermarkets now prepacked and ready to cook.

One of the reasons they have so little fat is that they need to be quick and agile as one of their favourite pastimes is staring down vehicles on local highways.

# Slow Cooker Kangaroo Curry

**Serves: 4**

*A delicious slow cooker curry that will leave them hopping for more.
Add curry powder to suit your taste – I use about 2 tablespoons
Keen's curry powder in this recipe.*

4 large potatoes
4 large carrots
2 onions
2 tablespoons oil
1kg diced kangaroo
2 x 400ml cans coconut milk
2 beef stock cubes
Curry powder, to taste

**Method:**
• Peel potatoes, chop into 4cm pieces.
• Peel carrots and onions, chop into 2cm pieces.
• Heat oil in a large frypan over a medium to high heat.
  Bounce the roo in and fry up in batches until browned.
• Place roo into slow cooker bowl. Chuck in the potatoes, carrots
  and onions.
• Mix together coconut milk, crumbled stock cubes and curry
  powder. Pour over meat and vegies, mix well.
• Cover with lid, cook on Low for 7 to 8 hours or High for 4 hours.
• Season well with salt and pepper.

*Serve with rice.*

# Kangaroo Shepherd's Pie

**Serves: 4**

*You can't go past a classic shepherd's–style pie with a hopping twist for a satisfying Sunday dinner.*

1 onion
1 carrot
2 stalks celery
4 potatoes *(800g)*
1 tablespoon olive oil
500g kangaroo mince
2 tablespoons plain flour
2 cups beef stock
1 tablespoon tomato paste
1 tablespoon Worcestershire sauce
3 tablespoons butter
¼ to ½ cup milk

**Method:**
• Peel and finely chop onion, carrot and celery.
• Peel potatoes and chop into quarters.
• Heat oil in a large saucepan over medium to high heat.
• Throw in your onion, carrot and celery, cook, stirring for 5 minutes.
• Hop the roo into the pan and fry up until cooked, stirring to break up any lumps.

- Sprinkle over flour, cook, stirring for 2 minutes.
- Gradually add stock, stirring until sauce boils and thickens.
- Stir in tomato paste and Worcestershire sauce, cover with lid, simmer for 30 minutes or until roo is tender. Season.
- Meanwhile, cook potatoes in a large saucepan of boiling, salted water until tender. Drain. Return to pan with 2 tablespoons of butter, mash well. Add the milk, mash until thick and creamy.
- Spoon roo mixture into a greased ovenproof dish (*8 to 10 cup capacity*). Top with mashed potato, use a fork to spread over.
- Melt remaining butter and brush over potato. Cook in oven at 200°C for 20 minutes or until golden brown.

# Italian-Style Slow Cooked Kangaroo

**Serves: 4**

*A beautiful stovetop meal perfect for winter.*

2 potatoes
2 carrots
1 onion
2 tablespoons olive oil
1kg diced kangaroo
2 teaspoons minced garlic
400g can crushed tomatoes
½ x 140g tube tomato paste
2 litres beef stock
40g sachet beef and red wine slow cooker recipe base
1 tablespoon Italian seasoning
400g can four bean mix

**Method:**
• Peel potatoes, carrots and onion, chop into 2cm pieces.
• Heat half the oil in a large saucepan over a medium to high heat.
• Throw the roo in and fry up in batches until browned. Remove from pan.
• Add the remaining oil to pan, cook onion and garlic for 3 to 4 minutes or until garlic is light golden.
• Return roo to pan with potatoes, carrots, tomatoes, tomato paste, stock, recipe base sachet and Italian seasoning, mix well.
• Bring to boil. Lower heat, cover with lid, simmer gently for 1 hour or until roo is tender. Drain and rinse beans well, add to pan. Simmer for a further 15 minutes.

*Serve with crusty bread or mashed potatoes.*

# Kangaroo Bagettie
**Serves: 4**

*An Indigenous take on a family classic that'll have the joeys skipping back for more.*

1 tablespoon olive oil
500g kangaroo mince
50g pkt Spaghetti Bolognese recipe base
700g tomato passata
400g spaghetti

**Method:**
- Heat oil in large saucepan. Add roo mince. (*Watch it don't bounce back out!*) Fry up for 5 minutes or until browned, stirring to break up any lumps.
- Stir in recipe base, passata and 1 cup of water. Bring to boil. Lower heat, cover with lid and simmer for 30 minutes.
- Meanwhile, cook spaghetti in a large saucepan of boiling, salted water according to packet directions, drain well.
- Serve sauce over spaghetti or add spaghetti to sauce in pan and mix well.

*Serve with grated cheese.*

# Seared Kangaroo with Broccolini

**Serves: 4**

*A simple and healthy meal. Serve with your choice of condiments.*

600g baby potatoes
1 bunch broccolini
2 cloves garlic
4 pieces kangaroo fillet *(about 125g each)*
Olive oil spray

**Method:**

- Wash and halve baby potatoes. Place in a steamer basket over a saucepan of boiling water. Cover and steam for about 10 minutes or until almost cooked. Lay broccolini over potatoes and steam a further 3 to 4 minutes or until vegies are cooked.
- Meanwhile, peel and crush garlic. Rub garlic all over roo fillets and season with pepper.
- Heat a large non–stick frypan over high heat. Spray with oil. Cook roo for about 4 minutes, turning occasionally until browned all over.
- Lower heat, cook for a further 2 minutes *(medium rare)*. Transfer to a plate and cover with foil. Leave to rest for 5 minutes.
- Thickly slice fillets across the grain. Serve with steamed potato and broccolini.

> *To avoid tough, chewy meat, don't overcook kangaroo – the centre should be pink. Let it rest for a few minutes after cooking.*

# Kangaroo Sizzle Steak Sandwich

**Serves: 4**

*Kangaroo is available in a variety of cuts in packs from the meat section of supermarkets.*

2 onions
2 tomatoes
¼ cup olive oil
¼ cup whole egg mayonnaise
2 teaspoons grain mustard
1 tablespoon chopped parsley
400g kangaroo sizzle steak
8 slices multigrain bread
1 cup rocket leaves

**Method:**
- Peel and slice onions.
- Slice tomatoes.
- Heat 2 tablespoons of oil in a frypan over a low heat. Toss in the onions and cook for about 8 minutes or until cooked. Remove from the pan.
- Meanwhile, mix together mayonnaise, mustard and parsley.
- Rub steaks with remaining oil. Heat frypan or barbecue on high heat.
- Cook steaks for 1 minute each side *(medium rare)*. Remove from heat.
- To assemble, toast bread and spread with mustard mayonnaise.
- Place cooked steaks on toast. Top with onions, sliced tomato, rocket and remaining slices of toast.

# Kangaroo Pastitsio

**Serves: 4 to 6**

*This recipe is made in two separate dishes so you can freeze one for later. Check one of the dishes is freezerproof before you start. If you like you can also make this in one large baking dish and cook a bit longer in the oven.*

400g pasta *(macaroni, elbow or penne)*
1 large onion
2 tablespoons olive oil
1kg kangaroo mince
2 teaspoons minced garlic
1 teaspoon ground cinnamon
½ cup red wine *(or water)*
2 tablespoons tomato paste
700g tomato passata
1 quantity white sauce *(see recipe page 237)*
¾ cup grated parmesan cheese

**Method:**
- Cook macaroni in a large saucepan of boiling, salted water. Drain well.
- Peel onion and finely chop.
- Heat oil in a large saucepan over a medium to high heat. Add roo mince in batches and fry up for 5 minutes or until browned, stirring to break up any lumps. Return all roo to pan.
- Add onion, garlic and cinnamon, cover with lid and cook for 5 minutes or until onion is softened.
- Stir in wine *(or water)*, tomato paste, passata and 1 cup water, simmer for 10 minutes *(or until sauce is rich and thick)*. Season.
- Meanwhile, cook white sauce. Stir in parmesan.
- Grease 2 x ovenproof dishes *(8 to 10 cup capacity)*.

- Divide macaroni over base of dishes.
- Spoon mince mixture over macaroni, then spread white sauce over the top. Cook one dish in oven at 180°C for 40 to 45 minutes or until golden brown.
- Allow the second dish to cool after assembling, cover in plastic wrap and freeze for another time.

# Kangaroo One Pan Dinner

**Serves: 4**

*A simple no–fuss dinner for when it's been one of them days.*

500g kangaroo mince
160g packet beef flavoured Dinner Winner
2 cups beef stock

**Method:**
- Heat a non–stick or lightly oiled frypan over a medium heat. Add roo mince and fry up for 5 minutes or until browned, stirring to break up any lumps.
- Throw in the contents of Dinner Winner packet, seasoning sachet contents and stock to the pan. Bring to a boil.
- Reduce heat and simmer uncovered for 15 minutes, stirring occasionally.

*TIP*

Serve on sliced bread for some madfeedz.

# Winter Warmer Roo Stew

**Serves: 4**

*A delicious hearty stew made with no added oil.*

3 potatoes
3 carrots
½ butternut pumpkin *(1kg)*
2 onions
3 salt–reduced beef stock cubes
750g diced kangaroo
1 teaspoon minced garlic
¼ cup oyster sauce
¼ cup salt–reduced tomato sauce
2 tablespoons cornflour

## Method:

- Peel potatoes and carrots, cut into 2cm pieces.
- Peel pumpkin, remove seeds, cut into 2cm pieces.
- Peel onions, chop into 1cm pieces.
- Pour 3½ cups water and the crumbled stock cubes into a large saucepan.
- Stir in roo, onions and garlic. Cover with lid and bring to a boil. Lower heat, simmer gently for 45 minutes.
- Chuck in the potatoes, carrots, pumpkin, oyster and tomato sauce. Add in enough water to almost cover the meat and vegetables. Bring to a boil, lower heat and gently boil for 20 minutes or until vegies are just cooked *(not soft).*
- Mix cornflour and ⅓ cup water together until smooth. Gradually add to pot, stirring until sauce boils and thickens. Gently boil for a further 2 minutes.

*Use extra cornflour if you want a thicker stew.*

# Roo Sausage Rolls

**Makes: 24**

*A perfect lunchbox snack for the joeys to take to school.*

1 onion
1 carrot
500g kangaroo mince
1 cup fresh breadcrumbs
¼ cup tomato sauce
1 teaspoon minced garlic
1 teaspoon mixed dried herbs
2 eggs
3 sheets frozen puff pastry, thawed

**Method:**
- Peel and finely grate onion and carrot. Place in a large bowl.
- Throw in the roo mince, breadcrumbs, tomato sauce, garlic, dried herbs and one of the eggs. Season with salt and pepper. Mix well.
- Using a large plastic zip lock bag, spoon mince mixture into bag and twist top. Cut an opening from one end of bag to squeeze out the mince mixture in a sausage shape.
- Place pastry sheets on chopping board. Cut each sheet in half lengthways.
- Pipe mixture down one long edge of each piece of pastry. Brush egg down the opposite long edge. Roll up to enclose filling.
- Cut each roll into four pieces. Place seam side down on two large oven trays lined with baking paper.
- Lightly beat remaining egg, brush over each roll.
- Cook in oven at 200°C for 20 to 25 minutes or until pastry is golden brown and filling is cooked.

*Serve with tomato or barbecue sauce.*

# Beef

Australia produces some of the highest quality beef in the world. Served as juicy grilled steaks, a tender roast or your own special creation, Aussie beef helps put delicious, crave–able meals on your family table all year long.

# Rump Steak with Mushroom Sauce

**Serves: 4**

*Amazing rump steak paired with a delicious mushroom sauce.*

4 x 150g rump steak medallions
500g "microwave in bag" mini white potatoes
1 onion
2 tablespoons olive oil
200g button mushrooms
2 tablespoons Worcestershire sauce
⅓ cup sour cream
2 tablespoons chopped parsley

**Method:**
- Cut steak into 4 portions.
- Slice mushrooms. Peel and finely chop onion.
- Throw the bag of potatoes into microwave and cook according to packet directions. Set aside covered to keep warm.
- Brush steak pieces with 1 tablespoon of the oil and season with salt and pepper.
- Heat ya favourite large non-stick frypan on a medium to high heat. Add steaks and cook for 3 to 4 minutes each side *(medium)* or until cooked to your liking. Transfer to a plate, cover with foil.
- Add onion and mushrooms to pan, cook for 4 to 5 minutes or until golden and brown *(like me, 'ey)*. Chuck in the Worcestershire sauce, sour cream and ⅓ cup water. Gently boil for 1 minute or until sauce is slightly thickened. Season with salt and pepper.
- Serve steaks topped with mushroom sauce, baby potatoes drizzled with remaining olive oil and sprinkled with parsley.

# Meatballs & Zoodles

**Serves: 4**

*A classic delicious beef meatball with a healthy side.*

1 small onion
¾ cup basil leaves
3 medium zucchini
500g lean beef mince
1 tablespoon olive oil
400g quality napolitana pasta sauce
¼ cup shaved parmesan

**Method:**
- Peel and chop onion into 1cm pieces.
- Finely chop ½ cup of the basil leaves.
- Put the zucchini through the spiralizer, set aside.
- Throw the mince, onion and chopped basil together into a large bowl. Season with salt and pepper, then roll into jawbreaker–size meatballs.
- Heat the oil in ya favourite large non–stick frypan over medium to high heat.
- Cook the meatballs for 6 to 7 minutes or until browned all over and smelling lubly.
- Chuck in the pasta sauce and ¼ cup water and simmer for 3 to 4 minutes or until meatballs are cooked through.
- Add the zoodles and toss to coat. Place meatballs and zoodles into bowls.
- Top with parmesan and remaining basil leaves.

# Meltingly Tender Beef Casserole

**Serves: 4**

*An easy to make beef casserole perfect for winter.*

1kg chuck steak or gravy beef
¼ cup olive oil
1 large onion
3 large potatoes
2 carrots
2 stalks celery
1 tablespoon plain flour
3 cups beef stock
¼ cup tomato paste
4 sprigs fresh thyme or rosemary

**Method:**
- Chop beef into 3cm pieces, add 2 tablespoons oil, season with salt and pepper, mix well.
- Peel onion, potatoes and carrots. Chop into 3cm pieces. Slice celery.
- Heat ya large frypan over a medium to high heat. Brown the beef in 2 or 3 batches. Remove each batch and chuck in an ovenproof casserole dish.
- Lower heat in pan, add remaining oil, onion, carrots and celery, cook for 3 to 4 minutes, stirring occasionally during the ad breaks on *Home and Away*.
- Sprinkle in the flour and stir until the vegetables are coated. Slowly pour in stock, add tomato paste, stirring well like ya stir up ya cousin after he fell up the stairs.
- Throw that lot in the casserole dish with the potatoes and herbs. Cover with lid.
- Cook in oven at 180°C for 2 hours or until beef is very tender. Stir occasionally, adding extra water if needed to keep the ingredients just covered.

*Serve with cooked peas or your favourite greens.*

# Beef Satay Skewers with Couscous

**Serves: 4**

*Beef skewers paired with a yummy satay sauce is a family favourite.*

500g thick beef steak *(rump, sirloin)*
1 yellow capsicum
250g cherry tomatoes
250ml bottle satay sauce
Olive oil spray
1 cup wholemeal couscous
Coriander leaves

**TIP**

If you are using bamboo skewers, soak them for 30 minutes in cold water before using to prevent burning.

**Method:**

- Chop beef and capsicum into 3cm pieces.
- Using 8 metal or bamboo skewers, thread beef, tomatoes and capsicum alternately onto skewers.
- Season with sea salt and pepper. Coat the skewers with half the satay sauce, leaving remainder of sauce for serving.
- Preheat a lightly oiled barbecue or chargrill pan over medium to high heat and cook skewers for 8 to 10 minutes, turning often, or until lightly charred and cooked through. Lubly lah!
- Meanwhile, prepare couscous according to packet instructions.
- Heat remaining satay sauce in a small saucepan or microwave.
- Serve the skewers drizzled with satay sauce and couscous sprinkled with coriander. Awwww deadly!

*Serve with baby salad leaves.*

# Beef Massaman Curry

**Serve: 4**

*Take the mob's tastebuds on an exotic trip with this beautiful
authentic slow cooked Thai curry dish.*

1kg chuck steak
1 large onion
500g desiree potatoes
2 tablespoons oil
¼ cup massaman curry paste
1 cinnamon stick
3 kaffir lime leaves
400ml can coconut milk
¼ cup fish sauce
1 tablespoon palm sugar
1 tablespoon lime juice

**Method:**
- Cut beef into 3cm pieces.
- Peel onion and finely chop. Peel potatoes and cut into quarters.
- Heat half the oil in a large frying pan over medium to high heat.
  Cook the beef, in batches until browned, about 5 to 6 minutes.
  Chuck into bowl of a 5 litre slow cooker.
- Heat remaining oil in pan and throw in the onion. Cook, stirring,
  for 5 minutes or until softened.
- Add paste, cook for 1 minute or until bubbling and fragrant,
  add to slow cooker with cinnamon, lime leaves, coconut milk,
  potatoes, fish sauce and sugar. Cover with lid. Cook on Low for 6
  to 8 hours or until beef is tender.
- Remove lime leaves and cinnamon stick and discard. Stir through
  lime juice.

*Serve with steamed rice and chopped peanuts.*

# Indian Curry Mince with Papadums

**Serves: 4**

*An Indian–inspired curry mince served on rice or saved for toast the next day. Lubly lah.*

1 onion
1 tablespoon vegetable oil
500g beef mince
⅓ cup korma curry paste
400g can diced tomatoes
165ml can coconut milk
2 Lebanese cucumbers
75g bag plain mini papadums

**Method:**
• Peel onion and finely chop.
• Heat oil in a large frypan over medium heat. Add onion and cook for 2 to 3 minutes or until slightly softened.
• Add mince, cook for 4 to 5 minutes, breaking it up with the back of a wooden spoon, until browned up real lubly.
• Stir in curry paste and cook for 1 minute.
• Pour tomatoes, coconut milk and ½ cup water over mince, stir well.
• Bring to a boil, lower heat and simmer for 5 minutes or until sauce has thickened. Season with salt and pepper.
• Meanwhile, cut cucumber into thin ribbons using a vegie peeler.

*Serve with cucumber ribbons, papadums and mango chutney.*

# Sweet Chilli, Soy and Sesame Beef Ribs

**Serves: 4**

*These deadly ribs will have the mob asking for seconds.*

10 to 12 beef short ribs
½ cup sweet chilli sauce
¼ cup tomato sauce
¼ cup soy sauce
2 teaspoons minced garlic
1 tablespoon crushed ginger
2 tablespoons toasted sesame seeds

**Method:**
- Place beef ribs in a stockpot, cover with water. Bring slowly to a simmer over a low heat, then simmer gently like ya aunty waiting for a number at bingo, partially covered for 1 hour.
- Remove ribs from water, drain well, cool slightly.
- Mix together chilli, tomato and soy sauces, garlic and ginger in a large bowl or dish. Add ribs and mix until well–coated with marinade. Stand for 30 minutes or marinate covered in refrigerator overnight.
- Barbecue ribs over a moderate heat for 10 to 12 minutes turning often and basting with any marinade until ribs are golden brown, cooked through and smelling mad as.
- Serve sprinkled with toasted sesame seeds.

**TIP**

Ask your butcher or meat manager at the supermarket about beef ribs. As a guide, serve 2 to 3 beef ribs per person.

# Three Cheese Beef Burger

**Serves: 4**

*The kids won't be asking for Micky D's after you knock this burger out.*

500g beef mince
¼ cup grated parmesan
⅓ cup chopped mozzarella
¼ cup grated smoked cheddar
4 ciabatta rolls with olives
2 tomatoes
1 red onion
1½ cups baby rocket leaves
⅓ cup tomato chutney

**Method:**
- Combine the mince, parmesan, mozzarella and cheddar.
- Season with salt and pepper. Shape into four burgers.
- Brush or spray burgers lightly with oil. Heat a large non–stick frypan over high heat – the burgers should sizzle when you add them to pan. Lower to medium heat and cook for 6 to 7 minutes on each side or until cooked through.
- Meanwhile, split rolls in half and slice tomatoes and onions thickly.
- Place rocket and tomato on roll bases, top with beef burger, chutney and onion. Replace roll tops.

*Serve with sweet potato fries.*

# Cowboy Steaks with Gravy

**Serves: 4**

*A classic old western! In the USA, they use flat iron steak – oyster blade steak is similar.*

¾ cup plain flour
1 tablespoon onion powder
2 teaspoons garlic powder
½ teaspoon sea salt
½ teaspoon freshly ground pepper
½ cup milk
1 egg
1 teaspoon Tabasco sauce
4 x 150g oyster blade steaks
2 tablespoons olive oil
165g pkt liquid brown onion gravy

**Method:**
- Whack the oven on to 200°C. Chuck flour, onion, garlic powder, salt and pepper in a shallow bowl.
- Whisk together milk, egg and tabasco sauce in another shallow bowl. Set aside.
- Using the tenderizing part of a meat mallet, flog the steaks out to 1cm thickness.
- Dip each steak in the egg mixture, then coat in the flour mixture.
- Place on a plate and refrigerate until ready to cook.
- Heat a large, heavy–based frypan over a medium heat. Add oil, cook steaks for 1 minute each side until golden and crisping up. Place steaks onto a baking tray lined with baking paper. Cook in oven for 5 minutes to finish cooking.
- Heat gravy according to packet directions, spoon over steaks.

*Serve with mashed potato or chips.*

# Corned Beef with Mustard Sauce

**Serves: 6**

*Who doesn't love corned beef? A classic homemade meal made deadly with this creamy sauce.*

1½kg corned beef silverside
6 pickling onions, peeled
2 bunches baby carrots
2 tablespoons brown sugar
2 tablespoons white wine vinegar
2 bay leaves
6 cloves
12 whole black peppercorns

**Mustard sauce**
60g butter
2 tablespoons plain flour
¼ cup cream
2 tablespoons wholegrain mustard
2 tablespoons finely chopped chives

**Method:**
• Trim excess fat from corned beef and discard, rinse beef well.
• Peel onions. Trim tops from baby carrots and peel.
• Place corned beef, sugar, vinegar, bay leaves, cloves, peppercorns and onions into a stockpot. Cover well with cold water, bring to a boil.

- Lower heat, simmer partially covered with lid for 1½ to 2 hours or until a fork easily penetrates the centre of beef. Add carrots to pot, simmer a further 5 to 10 minutes or until tender.
- Remove beef from pan, set aside until cool enough to handle. Strain liquid into a bowl, reserving onions and carrots.
- To make sauce: melt butter in a medium saucepan over medium heat. Stir in flour, cook for 1 minute, remove from heat, gradually stir in 2 cups of the cooking liquid.
- Cook over medium heat, stirring until sauce boils and thickens. Add cream and return to the boil. Stir in mustard and half the chives. Season.
- Slice beef thinly against the grain. Serve with mustard sauce, onions and carrots. Sprinkle with remaining chives. Deadly bow lah.

*Lubly cold on sandwiches with pickles and salad or cheese.*

# Pork

Pork is another amazing protein that is so versatile – smoked, grilled, slow cooked, steamed, baked, deep fried or spit roasted. In this chapter, I'll show you a couple of ways to get some more pork on your fork.

# Foolproof Roast Pork Belly
**Serves: 4**

*Delicious on its own or twice–cooked in your favourite marinade.*

1kg pork belly
1 tablespoon oil
1 tablespoon sea salt flakes
Freshly ground black pepper

**Method:**
- Get ya pork belly and pat dry with paper towel.
- With a small sharp knife, deeply score rind at 1cm intervals, but don't cut into the meat.
- Put the pork on a wire rack in the sink and pour a jug of boiling water over the rind.
- Pat dry really well with paper towel. Whack your oven to 240°C.
- Rub the rind with oil and salt *(more if you like salty crackling)*, making sure it penetrates the scores.
- Place the roast on a wire rack in a roasting pan. Cook in oven until the rind crackles like the time ya remind ya cuzzo you pushed him down the hill in a shopping trolley, about 50 minutes.
- Turn the oven down to 180°C and cook for a further 25 minutes or until cooked in the centre.
- Rest for 10 minutes before slicing up like Uncle Cliffy sliced up at Brookvale.

# Glazy Mango Pork

**Serves: 4**

*One of the best condiments you can keep in your fridge, mango chutney adds glaziness as well as a deadly flavour.*

4 large pork chops
1 teaspoon garlic powder
1 teaspoon onion powder
1 tablespoon olive oil
½ cup mango chutney
1 tablespoon soy sauce

## Method:
• Sprinkle pork chops with garlic and onion powder.
• Heat oil in ya large favourite frypan over a medium heat. Cook chops for about 3 minutes on each side or until golden brown.
• Add chutney and soy to pan with ½ cup water. Simmer for 2 to 3 minutes or until pork is cooked and glaze is lubly and thick.

*Serve with steamed rice or couscous.*

# Slow Cooked Pulled Pork

**Serves: 4 to 6**

*A delicious slow cooked meat best served on a fresh soft roll topped with some marinade. Use your favourite jars of marinade.*

1 to 1½kg piece pork neck
2 x 375g jars soy honey & garlic marinade

**Method:**
• Put the pork in an airtight container and pour in the marinade. After placing on the lid give it a shake to get the sauce underneath. Store in the fridge for 2 to 24 hours.
• Place pork in the slow cooker with the marinade. Cover with lid.
• Cook on Low for 8 hours or until pork is very tender.
• Use forks to shred the pork.

*I like to serve shredded pork on soft dinner buns with coleslaw topped with the sauce from the slow cooker.*

# Spicy Chinese BBQ Pork

**Serves: 4**

*A delicious restaurant–style meal that you can make at home. You will need to marinade the pork, so start this the night before.*

1kg pork fillets
½ cup char siu sauce
1 tablespoon oyster sauce
1 tablespoon light soy sauce
½ teaspoon Chinese five–spice powder
1 tablespoon minced garlic
1 tablespoon crushed ginger
½ teaspoon chilli powder *(optional)*

**Method:**
- Place pork in a large zip lock bag. Throw in all other ingredients. Seal bag and squish everything around to coat pork.
- Place in fridge for at least 6 hours *(ideally overnight)*.
- Place a metal rack into a roasting pan. Pour in water about 1 to 2cm deep. *(Don't let water touch rack.)* Place pork on rack, reserve marinade.
- Cook in oven at 200°C for 20 minutes. Remove and turn pork over. Brush with marinade. *(Make sure there is always a layer of water in pan).*
- Return pork to oven for a further 15 to 20 minutes or until cooked in centre.
- Meanwhile, tip any remaining marinade and ¼ cup water into a small saucepan and boil for 5 minutes, adding extra water if sauce starts to catch or get too thick.
- Rest pork 5 minutes. Spoon over sauce and cut into slices.

*Serve with rice or add to a salad.*

# Pork Sausage Curry

**Serves: 4**

*A classic family favourite that will win them over every time.*

2 large potatoes
1 large carrot
1 large onion
1 tablespoon oil
600g pkt pork sausages
400ml can coconut cream
1 to 2 tablespoons curry powder

**Method:**
• Peel and slice potatoes and carrot.
• Peel and slice up the onion like Souths slice up the competition.
• Heat oil in a large frypan over medium heat. Throw in ya pork sausages and onion and fry until the onion is lightly browned like me and sausages are cooked up enough to cut. Awwww lubly.
• Pull 'em off the heat, onto a plate and cut into bite−size pieces.
• Throw the pan back on the heat, chuck in the coconut cream, curry powder, potatoes, carrots and sausages.
• Stir it up like Bob Marley until sauce comes to a boil.
• Lower heat and simmer until vegetables and sausages are cooked, about 20 to 25 minutes.
• Season with salt and pepper.

*Serve with rice. #madfeedz*

# Crackling Pork Roast

**Serves: 8**

*A classic roast idea for the Sunday family get–together.*

2kg pork leg roast *(boneless)*
1 tablespoon vegetable oil
1 tablespoon sea salt

**Method:**
- Using a sharp knife, deepen scoring on rind and fat of pork, but do not cut through meat. Pat dry with paper towel.
  *(If time allows, leave the roast uncovered in the fridge for 1 hour, or ideally overnight. This helps dry out the rind more and aids the crackling process.)*
- When you're almost ready to cook, position rack in centre of oven and crank oven up to 240°C.
- Put your pork on a wire rack in the sink and pour a jug of boiling water over the rind. Drain off water and pat dry really well with paper towel.
- Rub oil and salt all over and into rind.
- Place pork in a large roasting pan. Cook in oven for 40 to 50 minutes or until rind has crackled and is crisp and blistered.
- Lower oven to 180°C, cook for a further 1 to 1¼ hours or until cooked through. *(A meat thermometer should read at least 70°C to 75°C in the centre of pork.)*
- Transfer pork to a carving board and set aside for 15 minutes to rest.

*Serve with apple sauce and roast vegies.*

# Pork & Ginger Honey Stir Fry

**Serves: 4**

*A delicious stir fry when you want a quick meal or the cuzzos rock up announced.*

500g pork stir fry strips
1 teaspoon minced garlic
1 tablespoon crushed ginger
2 tablespoons lemon juice
2 tablespoons honey
2 tablespoons soy sauce
2 tablespoons shao hsing
3 teaspoons cornflour
2 tablespoons vegetable oil
2 bunches broccolini, trimmed, halved

## Method:

- Throw together ya pork, garlic and ginger in a large bowl.
- Mix lemon juice, honey, soy sauce, shao hsing and cornflour in a jug.
- Heat half the oil in wok over high heat. Add half the pork, stir fry for 2 to 3 minutes or until browned. Repeat with remaining oil and pork.
- Throw ya pork back into wok with broccolini and cornflour mixture, stir fry for 2 to 3 minutes or until sauce boils and thickens and pork and broccolini are cooked.

*Serve with rice and have yourself some madfeedz.*

**TIP**

Shao hsing is Chinese cooking wine, available at supermarkets or Asian grocers.

# Simple Pad Thai
**Serves: 4**

*Takeaway at home – this will keep 'em happy for sure.*

200g pkt rice stick noodles
1 onion
3 spring onions
2 tablespoons vegetable oil
500g pork mince
240g jar pad thai paste
1 tablespoon crunchy peanut butter
1 tablespoon fish sauce
1 egg

## Method:
• Place noodles in a heatproof bowl. Pour over boiling water to cover. Leave for 3 minutes. Drain and rinse under cold running water. Drain.

• Meanwhile, peel onion, cut into thin wedges. Slice spring onions into 2cm lengths.

• Heat oil in ya large frypan or wok. Add pork, stir fry for about 5 minutes or until lightly browned, breaking up mince.

• Add onion, stir fry for 2 minutes. Add pad thai paste, peanut butter, fish sauce and ⅓ cup water. Stir fry for 1 minute.

• Add noodles, most of the shallots and stir through the lightly beaten egg. Cook stirring gently for 2 to 3 minutes or until noodles are heated through and egg is cooked.

*Serve with lemon wedges and fresh bean sprouts for added crunch.*

# Savoury Pork Mince
**Serves: 4**

*Definitely an old–time favourite, tastes better the next day or make a day before a corroboree cos ya know you'll be looking for this when you get home or wake up in the horrors the next day.*

400g desiree potatoes
1 large onion
200g button mushrooms
1 tablespoon olive oil
500g pork mince
2 tablespoons beef gravy mix
410g can tomato puree
200g button mushrooms
1 cup frozen peas, corn and carrot

## Method:
• Peel potatoes and onion and chop into 2cm pieces.
• Cut mushrooms into quarters.
• Heat oil in a large saucepan over medium–high heat. Add onion and mince, stirring with the Broncos' wooden spoon to break up mince, for 6 to 8 minutes or until golden brown like me.
• Throw in gravy mix, tomato puree and 1 cup cold water. When it starts simmering like ya cranky auntie, throw potato and mushrooms in.
• Once it's boiling like a land council meeting, lower heat, cover with a lid and simmer for 20 minutes or until potato is just tender. Season well.
• Chuck in peas, corn and carrot, cook for 5 minutes.

*Serve with rice or on heavily buttered toast.*

# Pizza Pork Steaks

**Serves: 4**

*Pork Hawaiian–style!*

1 green capsicum
1 tablespoon olive oil
4 pork loin steaks
⅓ cup BBQ rib sauce
227g can pineapple pieces in juice
4 slices cheddar or mozzarella cheese

**Method:**
- Chop capsicum into 1 to 2cm pieces.
- Heat oil in ya large frypan over a medium to high heat. Add pork, cook for 3 to 4 minutes each side or until golden brown.
- Place on a baking tray lined with baking paper and drizzle over rib sauce.
- Drain pineapple well, arrange capsicum and pineapple over steaks. Top with cheese.
- Cook in oven at 200°C for 5 to 6 minutes or until cheese has melted.

*Serve with rice or garlic bread. Awwww deadly!*

# Sweet Chilli Spare Ribs

**Serves: 4**

*Not the American-style ribs, these are the soft juicy spare ribs that melt in your mouth.*

1¼kg pork spare ribs
½ cup sweet chilli sauce
⅓ cup tomato sauce
⅓ cup soy sauce
2 tablespoons hoisin sauce

**Method.**
• Toss spare ribs and sauces together in a large bowl.
• Line a large roasting pan with baking paper. Place an oiled wire rack into pan. Lay spare ribs onto rack. Reserve remaining marinade.
• Cook in oven at 200°C for 25 minutes. Remove from oven and turn ribs over. Brush with some of the reserved marinade.
• Return to oven for a further 25 to 30 minutes, turning spare ribs and brushing with marinade once more during cooking or until spare ribs are well browned, glazed and cooked through.
• Meanwhile, place remaining marinade in a small saucepan with ½ cup water. Bring to a boil over a medium heat. Gently boil for 10 to 15 minutes or until sauce is reduced to a nice syrupy consistency.
• Place spare ribs on a serving plate and spoon over sauce.

*Serve with rice and steamed snow peas.*

# Arrabbiata Pork with Olives

**Serves: 4**

3 cloves garlic
200g mushrooms
2 tablespoons olive oil
750g pork schnitzel steaks
400g jar arrabbiata pasta sauce
⅓ cup white wine *(or water)*
½ cup pitted Kalamata olives
4 slices mozzarella cheese

**Method:**
- Peel garlic and finely chop. Slice mushrooms.
- Heat oil in a large frypan over medium to high heat. Cook pork in two batches for 1 minute each side or until light brown. Remove and cover pork with foil to keep warm.
- Add garlic and mushrooms to pan, add a little more oil if needed. Cook for 2 minutes or until mushrooms are slightly softened.
- Add pasta sauce, wine *(or water)* and olives. Boil for 1 minute. Return pork to pan and top with cheese. Simmer for about 1 to 2 minutes or until cheese has melted.

*Serve with crusty bread rolls, pasta or crispy baked potatoes.*

# Mexican Tray Bake

**Serve: 4**

*The kids are gunna love this one! Keep the salsa mild if they don't like the heat.*

750g packet frozen sweet potato chips
1 large onion
2 tablespoons olive oil
500g pork mince
400g can black beans
35g sachet taco seasoning mix
2 x 300g jars chunky tomato salsa
1½ cups grated pizza cheese

**Method:**
- Spread sweet potato chips over a large greased baking tray.
- Cook in oven at 200°C for 25 minutes or until golden.
- Meanwhile, peel onion and finely chop.
- Heat oil in ya favourite large frypan over high heat. Add mince and onion, cook stirring, for 5 minutes or until browned, breaking up mince.
- Drain beans, rinse well, add to mince with taco seasoning, both jars of salsa and ½ cup water. Gently boil for about 5 minutes or until mixture has thickened.
- Scatter chips over base of a large shallow ovenproof dish. Dollop over mince mixture.
- Sprinkle over cheese. Cook in oven at 220°C for 10 to 12 minutes or until cheese is melted and lubly.

*Serve with guacamole, sour cream and corn chips to really make a feast!*

# Lamb

Lamb! I hope I can make Lambassador Sam Kekovich proud in this section. Never lamb alone, whether you're chasing a lamb kebab at 2 am or throwing a lamb chop on the barbie at a celebration. It can be slow cooked, chargrilled, oven roasted, broiled or even stir fried – doesn't matter what way you make it, you'll love it.

# Slow Cooked Lamb Shanks in Red Wine

### Serves: 4

*The shanks are the best part, cooked low and slow until the meat is almost melting and falling off the bone. Making myself hungry typing this!*

2 onions
4 cloves garlic
2 tablespoons plain flour
4 lamb shanks *(about 400g each)*
¼ cup olive oil
2 cups red wine
800g can crushed tomatoes
2 tablespoons tomato paste
2 cups chicken stock
2 sprigs rosemary

### Method:

- Peel onions and garlic and finely chop.
- Sprinkle flour over a plate, sprinkle generously with salt and pepper. Coat shanks in flour.
- Heat 2 tablespoons of oil in ya large frypan pan over medium heat.
- Cook the lamb until brown all over, about 6 to 7 minutes. Place lamb in the bowl of a 5½ to 6 litre slow cooker.
- Add remaining oil, onion and garlic to frypan, cook until light golden, about 5 to 6 minutes.
- Stir in red wine, tomatoes, paste, stock and rosemary. Pour over lamb.
- Cover with lid. Cook on Low for 7 to 8 hours. Remove rosemary and discard.

*Serve with mashed potatoes. Lubly!*

# Lamb in Black Bean Sauce

**Serves: 4**

*A favourite of mine growing up. I've used lamb mince here but you can use sliced lamb steaks instead.*

2 bunches broccolini
2 tablespoons vegetable oil
750g lamb mince
2 teaspoons minced garlic
½ cup black bean sauce
⅓ cup honey
¾ cup roasted cashews

**Method:**

- Cut broccolini in half lengthways.
- Heat oil in a wok or large frypan over high heat. Add lamb and garlic in two batches, stir fry for 3 to 4 minutes or until cooked. Remove from wok.
- Add broccolini, black bean sauce, honey and ½ cup water to wok. Boil, stirring occasionally until broccolini is almost tender and sauce has slightly thickened, about 2 minutes.
- Return mince to wok with cashews and cook a further 1 minute.

*Serve over steamed white rice.*

# Gravylicious Lamb Chops

**Serves: 4 to 6**

*Who doesn't like lots of gravy? This one won't disappoint.*

¼ cup plain flour
1½kg lamb neck chops
2 large onions
¼ cup olive oil
3 teaspoons minced garlic
¾ cup white wine
400g can crushed tomatoes
2 large beef stock cubes

**Method:**

- Sprinkle flour over a plate, season well with salt and pepper.
- Coat lamb chops generously all over in flour. Reserve any leftover flour.
- Peel onions, halve and slice.
- Heat 2 tablespoons of the oil in ya favourite large frypan over a medium heat. Cook chops until golden brown on both sides. Place into bowl of a 5 to 6 litre slow cooker.
- Add remaining oil to pan, add onions and garlic, cook stirring until softened, about 5 to 6 minutes. Stir in any remaining flour from coating chops.
- Add wine, tomatoes, stock cubes and 1 cup water, bring to the boil. Pour over lamb.
- Cover with lid. Cook on High for 4 to 5 hours or until meat is really tender.

*Serve with hot cooked chips, mashed potatoes or fresh buttered bread. Lubly lah!*

# Turkish-Style Meatloaf

**Serves: 4**

*This meatloaf is as deadly as a bat out of hell! Uppercut them like Mungo with this lamb meatloaf.*

1 eggplant *(300g)*
1 onion
250g pkt microwave brown rice
¼ cup tomato paste
¼ cup chopped fresh dill
2 teaspoons cinnamon
2 teaspoons allspice
500g lamb mince
2 eggs
210g can chopped tomatoes

**Method:**
• Line a 12cm x 20cm loaf pan with baking paper and lightly oil.
• Finely chop eggplant. Peel and finely chop onion.
• Throw the onion and eggplant in a large bowl with rice, tomato paste, dill, cinnamon, allspice, lamb mince, eggs and 1 teaspoon each of salt and pepper. Mix together well with your hands.
• Tip the can of tomatoes into the base of the loaf pan. Pack the mince mixture on top and press down lightly to compact it.
• Cover the tin with foil. Cook in oven at 180°C for 1 hour. Remove foil and cook a further 15 minutes or until meatloaf is cooked in centre.

*Serve with potatoes, cooked any way you like!*

# Slow Cooker Madras Lamb Curry
**Serves: 4 to 6**

*Use your favourite curry paste in this slow cooker meal. You can use chopped chuck steak instead of lamb if you prefer.*

6 to 8 lean lamb steaks *(1kg)*
2 large onions
400g can chickpeas
½ cup Madras curry paste
2 x 400g can chopped tomatoes
¼ cup red lentils
2 tablespoons crushed ginger
1 teaspoon ground cumin
1 cinnamon stick
100g baby spinach leaves

**Method:**
• Remove any excess fat from lamb, chop into 3cm pieces.
• Peel onions, halve and slice. Drain chickpeas, rinse well.
• Chuck all ingredients *(except the spinach leaves)* and ½ cup water into the bowl of a 5 litre slow cooker and stir well. Cover with lid.
• Cook on Low for 6 hours or until the lamb is tender. Stir in spinach and cook a further 20 minutes or until spinach is cooked. Remove cinnamon stick.
• Season well with salt and pepper.

*Serve with cooked brown rice.*

# Mongolian Lamb

**Serves: 4**

*There are a few ingredients in this, but don't be put off, it's quick to cook and the first 6 ingredients get mixed together before you start!*

600g lamb leg steaks, trimmed, thinly sliced
2 tablespoons light soy sauce
2 tablespoons shao hsing wine
1 tablespoon cornflour
2 teaspoons minced garlic
1 tablespoon crushed ginger
1 large onion
2 green capsicums
2 tablespoons peanut oil
1 tablespoon oyster sauce
2 tablespoons hoisin sauce

**Method:**
- Thinly slice lamb steaks. Chuck in a bowl with soy sauce, shao hsing, cornflour, garlic and ginger, mix well. Place in refrigerator for 30 minutes.
- Meanwhile, peel onion, cut into thin wedges. Slice capsicums into 2cm pieces.
- Heat oil in a wok or large frypan over high heat. Add half the lamb, stir fry for 1 minute, remove from wok. Add remaining lamb and stir fry for 1 minute.
- Return all lamb to wok with remaining marinade, onion, capsicum, oyster and hoisin sauce, stir fry for 1 to 2 minutes or until sauce has bubbled and thickened and lamb is cooked.

*Serve with steamed white rice.*

# Samosa Pie

**Serves: 4**

*This Indian–inspired pie with mad spiced lamb mince, stewed potato
and peas topped with crispy filo pastry will have 'em asking for seconds.*

1 sweet potato *(300g)*
1 onion
3 tablespoons vegetable oil
500g lamb mince
2 teaspoons minced garlic
2 tablespoons curry powder
½ cup frozen peas
1 cup chopped coriander
2 teaspoons lemon juice
4–6 sheets filo pastry
1 teaspoon cumin seeds *(optional)*

## Method
- Peel sweet potato and grate. Peel onion and finely chop.
- Heat 1 tablespoon of oil in a frypan. Add onion and mince, cook
  stirring to break up mince for about 5 minutes until the meat is
  brown as me.
- Stir in sweet potato, garlic, curry and 1¼ cups water like ya stir
  Manly fans.
- Cook for 6 to 8 minutes until potato is as soft as the Dogs
  defence in the 2014 grand final.
- Stir in the peas, coriander and lemon juice. Season with salt and
  pepper.
- Spoon the mixture into an ovenproof dish *(8 cup capacity)*. Bung
  the oven on to 180°C.
- Brush each sheet of filo with remaining oil and scrunch up each
  one gently in your hands and place over the top of the mince.
  Sprinkle with cumin seeds.
- Cook in oven for 10 to 15 minutes or until the top is golden brown
  and crisp.

# Greek Lamb Gyros

**Serves: 4 to 6**

*Kebab shop quality made at home with beautiful slow–roasted Greek–inspired lamb that simply falls off the bone.*

4 cloves garlic
2kg lamb shoulder *(bone–in)*
2 fresh rosemary stalks
1 lemon
750g frozen chips
6 white soft wraps
200g tub tzatziki
Sliced tomato and lettuce

**Method:**
- Peel and halve garlic lengthways.
- Place lamb in a baking dish.
- Whack oven onto 180°C. Cut eight slits, 3cm deep into the lamb. Press one piece of garlic and a few green leaves of rosemary into each. Place lamb into a large roasting pan.
- Squeeze the juice from lemon all over lamb. Season with salt and pepper.
- Cook in oven for 2 hours. Cover and rest for 20 minutes. Slice or shred lamb.
- Meanwhile cook chips according to packet directions.
- Place chips on wraps among serving plates. Top with sliced or shredded lamb and tzatziki, tomato and lettuce, wrap up and eat!

*You can also add grated cheese to your gyros and sauce of your choice.*

# Classic Roast Lamb & Gravy

**Serves: 4**

*The ultimate Sunday lamb roast. Impress Mum when you make this for her.*

4 garlic cloves
1kg baby potatoes
1.6kg leg of lamb
¼ cup olive oil
2 tablespoons chopped rosemary leaves

**Wine Gravy**
2 tablespoons plain flour
1½ cups chicken stock
½ cup dry white wine *(or water)*

## Method:
• Peel garlic, halve cloves lengthways. Cut potatoes into halves.
• Cut eight slits, 3cm deep over the top of lamb. Press a piece of garlic into each, place lamb into a large flameproof roasting pan.
• Drizzle 1 tablespoon oil over lamb and sprinkle with rosemary leaves, salt and pepper. Cook in oven at 200°C for 15 minutes.
• Remove from oven, arrange the potato, in a single layer, around the lamb. Drizzle remaining oil over potato. Season. Return to oven for 1 hour *(for medium done)* or until lamb is cooked the way you like. Transfer lamb to a plate, cover.
• Turn potatoes over and return to oven for a further 10 minutes or until crisp. Place potatoes in a dish, cover with foil.
• To make gravy, place the roasting pan over medium heat. Sprinkle over flour, cook stirring until mixture turns light golden.
• Slowly add stock and wine, stirring until gravy boils and thickens.

*Serve lamb sliced with crispy potato and gravy. Have yaselves some deadly feeds, 'ey!*

# Rosemary & Garlic BBQ Lamb

**Serves: 4**

*Feed the mob fast with this deadly classic of rosemary and garlic lamb chops served with grilled vegetables.*

2 tablespoons orange juice

2 tablespoons red wine vinegar

2 teaspoons minced garlic

1 tablespoon chopped rosemary leaves

⅓ cup olive oil

8 lamb loin chops

3 zucchini

2 red capsicums

Store–bought salad *(potato or pasta works for me)*

**Method:**
- Mix together orange juice, vinegar, 1 teaspoon of the garlic, rosemary and half the oil in a shallow dish.
- Add the lamb chops, turn to coat. Set aside for 10 minutes.
- Fire up the barbecue grill or chargrill to medium to high heat.
- Meanwhile, slice zucchini and capsicum thickly. Toss with remaining oil and garlic.
- Cook vegies on grill plate, turning for 6 to 8 minutes or until tender and a lubly brown like me. Set aside.
- Cook lamb chops 3 minutes each side *(medium)* or until cooked how you like them. For the love of the Shire don't burn them.
- Season with salt and pepper and serve them suckers with the vegetables and salad.

# Lamb Kofta Kebabs

**Serves: 4**

*Kebab, kabob, kofta – whatever you call this, it's fragrant, it's exotic and it's fantastic for midweek because it's something different but so easy and fast to make.*

1 small onion
500g lamb mince
¼ cup finely chopped pistachio nuts
1 teaspoon salt
1 teaspoon ground black pepper
1 tablespoon ground cumin
1 tablespoon olive oil

**Yoghurt Sauce**
½ clove garlic
¾ cup Greek yoghurt
1 tablespoon lemon juice

## Method:

- To make Yoghurt Sauce, crush garlic, add to bowl with yoghurt and lemon juice. Season well with salt and pepper, cover and place in refrigerator.
- To make kebabs, peel and finely chop onion. Place in a bowl with mince, pistachios, salt, pepper and cumin. Mix well.
- Divide into 8 portions and mould onto skewers in a kofta shape.
- Heat oil in ya large frypan over medium to high heat. Add skewers a few at a time, cook for about 8 minutes until browned all over.

*Serve koftas and yoghurt sauce on pita bread, with store–bought tabbouleh. Wedges of lemon are also a great accompaniment. Awwww deadly!*

# Kleftiko-Style Lamb Shanks

**Serves: 4**

*This is a Greek–style lamb shank one pan dinner that's sure to please the mob. Lemon, oregano and feta mean it's full of deadly flavour.*

4 to 6 cloves garlic
1½kg potatoes
1 large red capsicum
4 to 6 lamb shanks *(about 400g each)*
3 teaspoons dried oregano leaves
½ teaspoon ground cinnamon
3 bay leaves
2 tablespoons olive oil
1 large lemon
½ cup dry white wine *(or water)*
150g Greek–style feta

**Method:**
- Peel garlic, roughly chop.
- Peel potatoes, cut potatoes and capsicum into 4cm pieces.
- Chuck lamb shanks into a large bowl with garlic, oregano, cinnamon, bay leaves and olive oil. Juice lemon and squeeze over. *(If you have time refrigerate lamb in marinade overnight.)*
- Whack the oven onto 190°C. Throw the potatoes and capsicum into a large roasting pan, pour over the wine *(or water)*. Remove lamb from marinade, pour marinade all over vegies.
- Place lamb shanks on top of vegies, cover tightly with foil, cook in oven for 2½ hours.
- Remove lamb from pan, turn vegies over. Turn lamb over and return to top of the vegies. Drizzle over a little more oil, if pan seems dry.
- Cook uncovered for another 30 minutes or until lamb is falling off the bone and the potatoes are looking lubly lah. Remove from oven, discard bay leaves.
- Rest lamb for 5 minutes, then crumble over feta.

# Sloppy Joe Lamb Curry Rolls

**Serves: 4**

*These spicy burgers can be topped with a fried egg to make them extra delicious!*

1 large onion
2 tablespoons vegetable oil
2 teaspoons minced garlic
1 tablespoon Keen's curry powder
500g lamb mince
1 tablespoon plain flour
400g can chopped tomatoes
1 tablespoon tomato paste
¼ cup fruit chutney
4 hamburger buns or rolls
Shredded lettuce, to serve
Sliced spring onions, to serve

**Method:**
• Peel onion and finely chop.
• Heat oil in ya large frypan over medium to high heat. Add onion, cook stirring for 3 minutes or until slightly softened.
• Stir in garlic, cook for 1 minute. Add curry powder and mince, cook stirring to break up mince for about 5 minutes or until browned.
• Sprinkle over flour, mix well. Stir in tomatoes, tomato paste, fruit chutney and ¾ cup water. Bring to a simmer, cook for about 20 to 25 minutes or until slightly thickened and nice and saucy. Season with salt.
• Split and toast hamburger buns, spoon lamb mixture over base of buns and top with shredded lettuce and sliced spring onions. Replace tops and serve.

# Fish & Seafood

What diet am I on? A see–food diet!
Seafood and fish have been a part of the Indigenous diet
since the start of time, whether it's fresh yellow belly,
yabbies from the river, oysters or fish fresh from the ocean.
And you can always guarantee that there'll be prawns at a
Koori gathering – if you forget them you'll be copping filthy
looks all day from Nan. Once I forgot them, never again!

# Possum's Tuna Mornay

**Serves: 4**

*A cheap, easy meal taught to me by my mother-in-law. She used to make it for my wife, and now I make it for her and the kids. It's a favourite in my household and hopefully it will be in yours, too.*

1 large onion
1 tablespoon butter
72g pkt *(2 minute)* instant noodles
425g can tuna in brine
420g can peas & corn
1 quantity white sauce *(see recipe page 237)*
  *(or 500g jar tuna bake sauce)*
¼ cup dried breadcrumbs
1 cup grated tasty cheese

## Method:

- Peel and chop onion finely. Throw into microwave–safe dish with butter and cook on High for 2 to 3 minutes, stirring once.
- Cook the noodles according to packet instructions. Drain and roughly chop.
- Drain tuna and peas and corn.
- Pour white sauce into an ovenproof dish *(8 to 10 cup capacity)*.
- Add onion, drained tuna, peas and corn and mix well, breaking up tuna.
- Stir in noodles, spread mixture evenly over dish.
- Sprinkle over breadcrumbs and cheese.
- Cook in oven at 190°C for 20 minutes or until golden.

# Creamy Garlic Prawns

**Serves: 4 to 5**

*This is an absolute favourite of mine – this lubly dish has been one of my go–to meals for years.*

3 cloves garlic
2 tablespoons butter
1 tablespoon olive oil
1 tablespoon plain flour
1 cup chicken stock
2 tablespoons white wine
½ cup cream
2 teaspoons Dijon mustard
750g peeled raw prawns, deveined
1 tablespoon chopped parsley

## Method

- Peel garlic and finely chop.
- Heat butter, oil and garlic in ya favourite medium frypan over medium until butter melts and garlic starts to cook.
- Throw in the flour. Cook, stirring for 1 minute or until mixture bubbles.
- Slowly add stock, ¼ cup at a time, stirring constantly to prevent lumps forming.
- Add in the wine, cream and mustard. Cook, stirring for 3 minutes or until sauce boils and thickens. Season with salt and pepper.
- Chuck in ya deadly prawns. Bring to a boil, lower heat and simmer, stirring for 3 to 4 minutes or until prawns are cooked through. Stir in parsley.

*Serve with steamed rice and enjoy them madfeedz!*

# Tuna Noodles

**Serves: 4**

*A simple, easy and cheap meal for the family. Use whatever flavoured tuna you like.*

5 x 72g pkts *(2 minute)* instant noodles
2 eggs *(optional)*
5 x 95g cans flavoured tuna

## Method
- Fill up a stockpot with water over a high heat and bring to a boil.
- Once water is boiling like ya nan because you made her tea wrong *(sorry, Nan)*, throw the noodle cakes in and boil until cooked. Drain noodles and return to dry pot.
- Throw in noodle seasonings and lightly beaten eggs, return to medium heat and stir it up like ya stir the Manly fans.
- When eggs are cooked, add in all the tuna and heat through.

*Enjoy some madfeedz!*

# Salmon Patties

**Serves: 4**

*These delightful flavoursome patties are a fantastic addition to a salad or served on a burger.*

1 onion
1 tomato
415g canned salmon
1 ½ cups mashed potato
½ cup cheese grated
1 egg
1 tablespoon lemon juice
1 tablespoon melted butter
1 cup dried breadcrumbs
1 teaspoon curry powder
2 egg whites
1 cup fresh breadcrumbs
Vegetable oil, for shallow frying

## Method

- Chop onion and tomato into 1cm pieces. Chuck into a large container with a lid.
- Add drained salmon, mashed potato, cheese, egg, lemon juice, butter, breadcrumbs and curry, mix well. Season with salt and pepper. Cover with lid.
- Place into the fridge for about 1 hour to chill.
- Remove from the fridge and roll heaped tablespoonsful of mixture into balls.
- Lightly whisk egg whites with a fork. Coat each ball in egg white, then roll in breadcrumbs.
- Heat oil in a large frypan over medium heat. Add balls in batches, flatten slightly in pan, cook until golden brown on both sides.
- Remove and place on paper towel to drain.

# White Wine Garlic Salmon

**Serves: 4**

*This is an absolute cracking meal to make if you want to impress.*
*It goes well with rice, steamed greens or a salad. Swap out the wine*
*for chicken stock or apple juice.*

3 to 4 cloves garlic
4 x 150g salmon fillets, skin on
1 tablespoon oil
2 tablespoons butter
1 cup dry white wine
1 to 2 tablespoons lemon juice
2 tablespoons chopped parsley

**Method:**
• Peel and finely chop garlic.
• Dry the salmon with paper towel, season and don't be stingy
  with the salt.
• Chuck ya favourite big frypan over a high heat, making sure it's
  nice and hot.
• Add oil and carefully place salmon in the pan, skin–side down,
  lower heat to medium high.
• Cook the salmon for 3 to 4 minutes until the skin is golden
  brown and crispy then flip 'em over.
• Cook for another 1 to 2 minutes on the flesh side until the
  salmon is almost cooked through. Pull 'em outta the pan and let
  'em rest.
• Melt the butter in the pan and add the garlic.
• Fry up until smelling lubly, then add wine (*or stock or juice*) and
  lemon juice.
• Simmer for 4 to 5 minutes or until reduced enough to make a
  thin sauce. Add the parsley and season to taste with salt and
  pepper.
• Return salmon to pan and baste with the sauce, cook gently
  until salmon is heated through and cooked as you like it.

# Baked Fish with Lemon Cream Sauce

**Serves: 4**

*This deadly one pan baked fish dinner has a lubly lemon cream sauce.*

2 cloves garlic

4 x 180g *(skinless and boneless)* barramundi fillets

50g unsalted butter

¼ cup thickened cream

1 tablespoon Dijon mustard

2 tablespoons lemon juice

2 tablespoons finely chopped eschallots

2 tablespoons fresh chopped parsley

**Method**

• Peel and finely chop garlic.

• Turn up the oven to 200°C like ya turn up Charlie Pride.

• Place fish in a large greased ovenproof dish, don't just jam them in, they need room to move dere!

• Sprinkle both sides of fish with salt and pepper.

• Place butter, cream, garlic, mustard, lemon juice, salt and pepper in a microwave–proof jug or bowl.

• Then throw it in the microwave for 2 x 30 second bursts, stirring in between, until melted and smooth.

• Sprinkle fish with eschallots, then cover the fish with the sauce, ahhh lubly!

• Cook in oven for 10 to 12 minutes, or until fish is cooked.

• Remove from oven and place fish onto serving plates. Spoon over sauce and sprinkle with parsley.

*Goes mad with rice or a salad.*

# Fish Curry
**Serves: 4**

*Amazingly simple and cheap meal that'll keep the family happy and swimming back for seconds.*

800g basa or firm white fish fillets
2 tablespoons coconut oil
2 tablespoons Thai red curry paste
2 onions
4 tomatoes
2 teaspoons curry powder
400g can coconut milk

## Method
- Cut fish fillets into 2 to 3cm pieces.
- Mix fish pieces, half the coconut oil and curry paste together in a bowl. Refrigerate.
- Peel and roughly chop onions. Chop tomatoes into 2cm pieces.
- Heat a large frypan over medium heat. Add remaining coconut oil and onions, cook until onions have softened, about 5 minutes.
- Throw in your curry powder and cook for 1 minute.
- Throw in the diced tomatoes, coconut milk and marinated fish and simmer for 5 minutes or until fish is cooked. Season well with salt.

*Serve with warm rice and lemon wedges.*

# Cheesy Salmon Pie
**Serves: 4**

*This simple pie will keep the tots happy on a cold winter's night.*

500g deboned, skinless salmon fillets
1 leek
2 stalks celery
50g butter
2 tablespoons plain flour
1 cup chicken stock
¼ cup cream
½ cup frozen peas
2 tablespoons grated cheddar cheese,
1 teaspoon dried tarragon
1 teaspoon finely grated lemon rind
1 sheet ready rolled puff pastry, just thawed
1 egg

**Method:**
• Cut salmon into bite size pieces.
• Wash leek well and thinly slice. Thinly slice celery.
• Crank up that oven to 220°C.
• Melt butter in a large saucepan over medium heat.
• Add leek and celery, throw the lid on, stirring occasionally, for about 10 minutes or until softened.
• Sprinkle over flour and cook, stirring, for 1 minute.
• Slowly stir in chicken stock and cream until as smooth as that one uncle y'all have.
• Add salmon, peas, cheese, tarragon and lemon rind. Gently boil for 3 to 4 minutes or until fish is just cooked. Season with salt and pepper.
• Fill pie dish with filling then place pastry sheet over pie dish

and press onto edge of dish to seal. Trim excess pastry off from around edge with a small sharp knife.

- Brush with lightly beaten egg. *(You can use the pastry cut–offs to decorate the pie if ya wanna be fancy, then brush with egg.)*
- Cook in oven for about 20 to 25 minutes or until the pastry is golden and puffed like me. Stand for 5 minutes before serving.

# Curried Prawns

**Serves: 2 to 3**

*Curried prawns have been a favourite of mine for years. A quick, simple meal to prepare, you can fancy it up by adding other ingredients but I like to keep it simple.*

400ml can coconut milk
1 tablespoon curry powder
500g peeled raw prawns

**Method**
- Pour the coconut milk into a large saucepan over a medium heat. When hot *(not boiling)* throw in curry powder, mixing well.
- Simmer for 4 to 5 minutes or until sauce is slightly thickened, stirring often so sauce doesn't stick.
- Add prawns and bring to a boil. Lower heat and simmer for 3 to 4 minutes or until prawns are cooked. *(Be careful not to overcook.)* Season with salt and pepper.

*Serve with rice and fresh lemon wedge. Lubly!*

# Vegies & Salads

These vegetables and salads are a fantastic side dish idea or brilliant on their own. Recipes suitable for vegetarians are marked with a **(V)** and those suitable for vegans with a **(VG)**. * is next to any ingredient you may need to check to make sure the brand is vegetarian or vegan friendly.

# Creamy Cheesy Potato Bake
**Serves: 10 (V)**

*This easy cheesy potato dish is true to its name.*

1¼kg potatoes
2 large cloves garlic
⅔ cup milk
¾ cup thickened cream
⅓ cup whole egg mayonnaise
2 teaspoons chopped fresh thyme leaves
2 cups shredded tasty cheese
1 cup shredded mozzarella cheese

## Method:
- Peel and cut the potatoes into 2cm cubes. Place in a large bowl.
- Peel and finely chop garlic, add to potatoes, with all remaining ingredients except the mozzarella cheese. Season with ¾ teaspoon salt and lots of freshly ground pepper.
- Pour into a large greased ovenproof dish (*12 cup capacity*). Cover with foil.
- Cook in oven at 180°C for 1 to 1¼ hours, or until potatoes are tender. Remove the foil, sprinkle over mozzarella cheese.
- Cook for 25 minutes or until the cheese is golden and lubly.
- Leave for 5 to 10 minutes before serving.

## To Make Ahead:
- Cook until potatoes are tender, remove from oven, cover and cool, refrigerate.
- Then either cover and microwave 5 to 8 minutes to reheat or cook in oven at 180°C for 20 to 30 minutes. Lastly, sprinkle with the mozzarella cheese and cook in oven uncovered until cheese is golden.

*Have yaselves some madfeedz!*

# Balsamic Roasted Mushrooms
## Serves: 4 (V) (VG)
*Roasted mushrooms are an easy side dish or appetiser, soaked in garlic, herbs and tangy balsamic vinegar for maximum flavour.*

500g mushrooms
2 cloves garlic
1 tablespoon olive oil
¼ cup balsamic vinegar
2 teaspoons brown sugar
1 tablespoon soy sauce
¼ teaspoon dried thyme leaves

## Method:
• Fire up the oven to 200°C. Slice any large mushrooms in half, you can leave them whole if they are small.
• Peel and finely chop garlic.
• In a small bowl toss together garlic, olive oil, balsamic vinegar, brown sugar, soy sauce, thyme and season with pepper. Place the mushrooms in an ovenproof dish. (*Choose a size that keeps the mushrooms close together, mostly in a single layer.*)
• Pour the marinade over top and stir to coat the mushrooms.
• Roast the mushrooms for about 45 minutes, stirring every 15 minutes. If the liquid in dish dries up in the last 15 minutes, cover the dish with foil to prevent burning.

*Serve sprinkled with chopped parsley.*

# Mushrooms Sautéed with White Wine & Garlic

**Serves: 6 (V) (VG)**

*An easy and delicious side dish for steak. Top with fresh chives.*

750g mushrooms
2 cloves garlic
1 tablespoon olive oil
⅓ cup dry white wine*
2 tablespoons chopped fresh chives

**Method:**
- Slice mushrooms if they are large or cut in half. Peel and crush garlic.
- Heat oil in a large frypan. Add mushrooms and cook for 10 minutes or until softened, stirring frequently.
- Add wine and garlic and cook until most of the wine has evaporated. Season with salt and pepper and sprinkle with chives. Cook for 1 more minute. Lubly lah!

# Satay Sweet Potato Curry
**Serves: 4 (V) (VG)**
*Cook this tasty vegetable curry for an exotic yet easy family dinner.*

500g sweet potato
1 onion, chopped
2 cloves garlic
Thumb–sized piece ginger
1 tablespoon coconut or olive oil
¼ cup Thai red curry paste*
1 tablespoon peanut butter
400ml can coconut milk
200g baby spinach leaves
1 lime

## Method:
• Peel and chop sweet potato into 3cm chunks.
• Peel and finely chop onion and garlic. Peel ginger and finely
  grate.
• Heat oil in a large saucepan over a medium heat. Throw in onion
  and cook for 5 minutes or until softened.
• Chuck in garlic and ginger and cook for 1 minute or until smelling
  lubly lah.
• Stir in curry paste, peanut butter and sweet potato, cook stirring
  for 1 minute.
• Pour in coconut milk and 1 cup of water. Bring to a boil, lower
  heat and simmer, uncovered, for 25 to 30 minutes or until the
  sweet potato is tender *(not mushy)*.
• Stir through 200g spinach and squeeze in the juice of lime.
  Season with salt and pepper.

*Serve with steamed rice.*

# Roasted Root Vegetables
## Serves: 4 (V) (VG)

 *You can use this basic guide for roasting vegetables with any root vegetables you prefer. Perfect with roast chicken or beef.*

1kg mixed root vegetables *(potatoes, sweet potatoes, carrots, parsnips)*
250g small onions or eschallots
2 tablespoons extra virgin olive oil
1 teaspoon cracked black pepper
Few sprigs fresh thyme
Few sprigs fresh rosemary

**Method:**
- Scrub or peel the root vegetables. Halve or quarter large potatoes.
- Cut large carrots or parsnips in half lengthways, then cut the pieces across in half again. Cut sweet potato into 4 to 5cm pieces. Leave onions or eschallots whole.
- Place all the vegetables into a stockpot and pour in enough boiling water to cover them. Bring back to a boil, lower heat and simmer for 5 to 7 minutes or until the vegetables are lightly cooked, but not yet tender.
- Crank that oven up to 220°C.
- Drain the vegetables and place them in a large oiled roasting pan. Brush or drizzle the vegetables with olive oil and sprinkle with salt and the pepper. Chuck the herb sprigs in the pan amongst the vegies.
- Cook in oven for 30 to 35 minutes or until the vegetables are golden–brown and tender, turning once during cooking.

# Broccoli Cheesy Rice Bake

**Serves: 6 (V)**

 *A creamy broccoli cheddar casserole from scratch. Rich, cheesy comfort food at its best!*

500g fresh broccoli florets
4 cups white or brown cooked rice
2 cups shredded Colby cheese
1 onion
2 cloves garlic
50g butter
¼ cup plain flour
2 cups milk
½ teaspoon smoked paprika
Good pinch cayenne pepper

**Method:**
- Wash broccoli and chop into 3 to 4cm pieces. Chuck into a large bowl with rice and 1½ cups of the cheese.
- Peel and finely chop onion and garlic.
- Crank the oven up to 180°C.
- Melt butter in a medium saucepan, add onion and garlic and cook over medium heat for 2 to 3 minutes or until onions are slightly softened.
- Sprinkle over flour, stirring until smooth and bubbling. Cook stirring for 1 minute.
- Gradually whisk in milk, continue whisking until sauce is gently bubbling and thickened. Boil gently for 1 to 2 minutes, stirring.
- Stir in smoked paprika and cayenne and ½ teaspoon salt. Season with pepper.
- Pour the sauce into the rice and broccoli mixture and stir until all the ingredients are evenly coated in sauce.

- Spread mixture into a greased ovenproof dish *(8 to 10 cup capacity)* and sprinkle over remaining shredded cheese.
- Cook in oven for about 35 minutes or until cheese is melted and golden brown. Divide into six lubly portions and serve.

# Miso Soy Broccolini
**Serves: 4 (V) (VG)**

*A quick, healthy and delicious snack or side dish.*

4cm piece fresh ginger
3 cloves garlic
2 tablespoons white miso paste
2 tablespoons vegetable oil
1 tablespoon soy sauce
¼ teaspoon dried chilli flakes *(optional)*
2 bunches broccolini

**Method:**
- Peel ginger and garlic and finely chop.
- Bring a large saucepan of water to a boil.
- In a large bowl, whisk together ginger, garlic, miso paste, oil, soy sauce and chilli flakes and season with black pepper.
- Drop broccolini into boiling water, cook for 1 to 2 minutes or until just tender.
- Drain well and toss with the miso mixture until broccolini is well coated. Serve immediately.

# Quick Vegie Tofu Stir Fry
**Serves: 4 (V) (VG)**
*This super fast and inexpensive tofu stir fry is so filling, easy enough for busy weeknights and endlessly customizable!*

¼ cup soy sauce
2 tablespoons brown sugar
1 teaspoon toasted sesame oil
1 teaspoon crushed ginger*
1 teaspoon minced garlic*
2 spring onions
350g extra firm tofu
2 tablespoons oil
200g bag fresh stir fry vegetables *(or coleslaw mix)*
¼ cup chopped peanuts

## Method:
- In a bowl, mix together soy sauce, brown sugar, sesame oil, ginger, garlic and 2 tablespoons of water.
- Cut spring onions diagonally into thin slices.
- Drain away excess moisture from tofu. Crumble tofu into a bowl.
- Heat oil in a wok or large frypan over medium to high heat. Add tofu and stir fry for 5 minutes, or until there is no longer any water in the bottom of the wok.
- Chuck in the prepared soy sauce mixture and stir fry for 2 to 3 minutes or until sauce is slightly thickened.
- Add stir fry vegetables and peanuts, stir fry for 1 to 2 minutes or until the vegetables just begin to soften slightly.

*Sprinkle over sliced shallots and a drizzle of chilli sauce, then serve them madfeedz!*

# Best Ever Potato Salad

**Serves: 10 to 12**

*So tasty, this potato salad will have everyone begging you for the recipe!*

2kg desiree potatoes
6 eggs
8 rashers short cut rindless bacon
1 bunch spring onions
440g jar whole egg mayonnaise
1½ teaspoons onion salt
1 tablespoon garlic powder

## Method:

- Peel or wash potatoes. Cut into 3cm cubes and place in a large stockpot and cover with salted water.
- Bring to boil, cook for 10 minutes or until the potatoes are just cooked when pierced with a knife, not falling apart. Drain and refrigerate for 2 hours.
- Meanwhile, place eggs in a medium saucepan and cover well with water. Bring to boil over high heat, cook for 8 to 10 minutes.
- Drain eggs and cool under running water until warm, then place eggs in a bowl of water in fridge for about 1 hour or until cold.
- Meanwhile, heat a frypan over high heat and cook bacon so it is browned but not too crispy. Drain on a paper towel and cut into thin pieces.
- Chop the spring onions into ½cm slices.
- Peel eggs and cut into quarters.
- Mix together mayonnaise, onion salt and garlic powder in a large bowl. Add potatoes, eggs, ¾ of the spring onions and bacon and mix well. Sprinkle remaining spring onions over top.

# Greek Salad

**Serves: 4 (V)**

*Yassou! Master this absolute classic and you'll never be short of a delicious lunch. The key to an authentic Greek flavour is plenty of oregano and red wine vinegar.*

3 Lebanese cucumbers
1 small red onion
4 tomatoes
20 pitted Kalamata olives
¼ cup extra virgin olive oil
2 tablespoons red wine vinegar
150g Greek–style feta, crumbled
½ teaspoon dried oregano leaves

## Method:

- Cut the cucumbers in half lengthways, scrape out the seeds with a teaspoon then cut into thick slices.
- Peel onion, cut in half and thinly slice. Chop tomatoes into chunks.
- Chuck the cucumber, onion, tomatoes and olives in a large shallow bowl. Whisk together the oil and vinegar, and season with salt and pepper.
- Pour most of the dressing over the salad and gently toss. Add the feta, drizzle over the rest of the dressing, then sprinkle over the oregano.

*Serve with crusty bread!*

# Spicy Cuey
**Serves: 1 to 2 (V) (VG)**

*A quick spicy snack perfect for lunch.*

1 cup white vinegar
¾ cup sugar
½ cup water
1 teaspoon sea salt
1 continental cucumber
½ long red chilli

## Method:
- Chuck vinegar, sugar, water and salt in ya medium saucepan.
- Cook stirring over a low heat until sugar and salt are dissolved. Set aside to cool.
- Meanwhile, thinly slice cucumber. Remove seeds from chilli and thinly slice. Place cucumber and chilli into a bowl.
- When vinegar mixture has cooled to warm, pour over cucumbers and chilli and marinade for 15 minutes in fridge.

*If you aren't into chilli, replace it with half a sliced red capsicum or white onion and some fresh chopped dill.*

# Warm Roasted Vegetable Salad

**Serves: 4 (V) (VG)**

*A wonderful salad perfect for a winter BBQ that's just a tad fancy.*

500g baby potatoes
4 cloves garlic
1 large sweet potato *(500g)*
1 large red capsicum
1 large red onion
¼ cup extra virgin olive oil
¼ cup toasted pine nuts
2 tablespoons lemon juice
2 teaspoons Dijon mustard
1 tablespoon chopped oregano leaves *(or 1 teaspoon dried)*
80g baby rocket leaves

**Method:**
• Wash and cut potatoes into halves. Peel garlic cloves.
• Peel sweet potato and chop into 4cm pieces.
• Cut capsicum into thick slices. Peel onion and cut into thick wedges.
• Bung the oven up to 220°C.
• Chuck the potato, sweet potato, whole garlic cloves and 2 tablespoons of the olive oil into a large roasting pan and toss together. Arrange in a single layer.
• Season with salt and pepper. Cook in oven for 25 minutes.
• Remove from oven and turn potato and sweet potato. Add capsicum and red onion to pan and return to oven to cook for 15 minutes.
• Sprinkle over pine nuts and cook for a further 5 minutes or until vegetables are browned and tender and looking deadly as.
• Meanwhile, make the dressing, place the lemon juice, remaining oil, mustard and oregano into a screw–top jar. Secure lid as tight as ya uncle on pay day and shake well to combine.

• Launch the rocket, vegetables and pine nuts into a large salad bowl.
• Pour over dressing. Toss gently to combine. Serve it up while listening to some Patsy Cline.

# Cuey Salad

**CHEAP EATS**

**Serves: 1 to 2 (V) (VG)**
*A perfect side dish for steak or fish.*

2 continental cucumbers
1 small red onion
1 tablespoon sea salt
2 tablespoons rice wine vinegar
2 teaspoons caster sugar
2 tablespoons fresh dill *(or 2 teaspoons dried dill)*

**Method:**
• Slice cucumbers lengthways and scoop out the seeds with a teaspoon. Cut into thin slices and chuck in ya large bowl.
• Peel and thinly slice onion, add to bowl.
• Toss the cucumber and onion together with the salt and transfer to a colander to drain for 20 minutes.
• Press out the liquid and rinse with cold water, drain well.
• In a serving bowl, mix together vinegar and sugar, add the cucumber mixture and toss well to coat.
• Sprinkle the dill over the top.

# Chicken Caesar Salad

**Serves: 4**

*This well–known salad is perfect for any time of the year and extra flavourful with bacon and chicken.*

1 cos lettuce
2 chicken breast fillets *(500g)*
250g bacon rashers
1 tablespoon olive oil
½ cup Caesar salad dressing
⅓ cup grated parmesan cheese
1 cup croutons

## Method:

- Wash, dry and cut lettuce into about 2cm thick slices.
- Slice chicken fillets into thin strips.
- Heat a large frypan over medium heat, cook the bacon until browned up lubly like me. Cool and cut into pieces.
- Wipe out the frypan, add oil and heat over medium to high heat. Cook chicken in two batches until golden brown and cooked through. Remove from frypan and drain on paper towel.
- Throw the lettuce, salad dressing, parmesan, bacon and croutons together in a large salad bowl. Top with the sliced chicken and serve.

# Chicken & Apple Salad

**Serves: 8**

*This salad has a lovely mix of fruit and vegetables and a little curry
powder for some zing. Even better if you can make it a day ahead.*

2 stalks celery
2 spring onions
2 red or green apples
2 cups chopped cooked chicken breast
¼ cup chopped walnuts
¼ cup lite mayonnaise
¼ cup plain fat–free yogurt
⅓ cup lemon juice
½ teaspoon curry powder

**Method:**
• Chop celery and spring onions into 1 to 2cm pieces. Remove core
  from apples and chop into 2cm pieces.
• In a medium bowl, combine the chicken, celery, spring onions,
  apple and walnuts.
• In a small bowl, whisk together the mayonnaise, yogurt, lemon
  juice, curry powder and season with salt and pepper. Add to the
  chicken mixture and gently stir to coat.

*Serve salad over lettuce leaves with bread or crackers.*

# Pasta & Bagettie

Pasta comes in so many different shapes, styles and textures, it should be a household staple. So many amazing cheap eats and gourmet meals can be kicked off using pasta, whether it's just pasta and sauce or kids making fresh pasta with Nonna. It's a connection to family and great food. What's Bagettie? It's spaghetti that's just been mispronounced by the kids.

# Easy Feta Pasta

**Serves: 4**

*Here's how to make that viral TikTok trend. Throw your own spin on this viral hit.*

4 rashers rindless bacon
500g cherry tomatoes
8 cloves garlic
1 teaspoon dried oregano leaves
¼ cup extra virgin olive oil
200g block feta cheese
400g small pasta *(I use orecchiette)*
Large handful fresh basil leaves

## Method:

- Crank that oven to 200°C. Cut bacon into 2cm pieces.
- Chuck the bacon, tomatoes, unpeeled garlic cloves and ½ the oregano in an ovenproof dish. Season with salt and pepper and drizzle over 2 tablespoons of the olive oil. Get in with your hands and give the ingredients a good mix.
- Place the block of feta cheese in the middle of the dish and move the other ingredients around it. Sprinkle remaining oregano over feta and drizzle over remaining olive oil.
- Cook in oven for 25 to 30 minutes or until tomatoes have blistered and feta cheese has softened.
- When there is about 10 minutes left of cooking time, cook pasta in a large stockpot of boiling, salted water. Drain. (*Save about ½ cup cooking water.*)
- Remove dish from oven and gently peel garlic cloves from their skin. Use a fork to mash garlic in the dish. (*Be careful, they will be hot.*)
- Give it all a mix together breaking up the feta cheese. It will become a nice, sauce–like consistency. Throw in the cooked pasta along with the basil leaves and mix together, if needed add a splash of cooking water to loosen the sauce.

# Spaghetti with Garlic & Olive Oil
**Serves: 4**

*A cheap and easy meal, the family will love.*

450g spaghetti *(or other long pasta)*
4 to 5 cloves garlic
½ cup extra virgin olive oil
1 teaspoon dried chilli flakes
⅓ cup fresh chopped parsley
⅓ cup grated parmesan cheese

## Method:
- Cook spaghetti in a large stockpot of boiling, salted water until al dentè. *(The spaghetti should be tender but still have a little chewy bite in the centre.)*
- Drain spaghetti. *(Save about ½ cup of the cooking water.)*
- Meanwhile, make the sauce, peel and finely slice the garlic cloves.
- Heat oil in a large frypan over a low to medium heat. Add garlic and chilli, cook gently for 2 to 3 minutes or until garlic is a pale golden colour. Stir in chopped parsley.
- Add spaghetti to frypan, stir well to coat with oil. Add a little of the reserved cooking water so that sauce is glossy.
- Return pan to a medium heat for 30 seconds or until heated through.
- Sprinkle with chopped parsley and parmesan cheese.

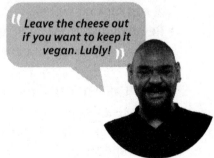

*Leave the cheese out if you want to keep it vegan. Lubly!*

# Pasta with Peas

## Serves: 4

 *This Italian pasta with peas is a simple, creamy and delicious one–pot dinner recipe that uses minimal ingredients. It makes a perfect weeknight meal that's ready in 15 minutes. Chuck in some diced ham, devon, bacon or pancetta with the onion if you want to bulk it up.*

1 small onion
2 tablespoons olive oil
450g fresh or frozen peas
2¼ cups vegetable stock or water
250g short shaped pasta *(ditalini, shell, elbow)*
½ cup grated parmesan cheese

## Method:

• Peel onion and finely chop.
• Heat oil in a stockpot over medium heat. Throw in the diced onion and cook about 4 to 5 minutes or until onion has softened.
• Chuck in the peas and cook stirring frequently for about 1 minute.
• Pour in stock *(or water)* and bring to a boil. Stir in pasta and salt to taste.
• Lower heat, cover with a lid and simmer pasta until all the stock is absorbed, Stirring frequently, otherwise it will stick to the bottom. *(Add extra stock or water gradually only if needed.)* Cook until pasta is al dentè
• Turn off the heat and stir in parmesan cheese until melted. Season with salt and black pepper.

*Serve with a drizzle of olive oil and extra parmesan cheese. Enjoy!*

# Easy Lemon Ricotta & Spinach Pasta

**Serves: 3**

*A beautiful flavoursome meal with some lemon zing.*

1 lemon
1 clove garlic
220g pasta *(spaghetti, linguine, penne, fusilli ...)*
1 cup ricotta cheese
1 tablespoon extra virgin olive oil
⅓ cup grated parmesan cheese
200g fresh baby spinach leaves

**Method:**
- Finely grate rind lemon, halve and juice. Peel garlic and crush.
- Cook pasta in a stockpot of boiling, salted water until al dentè.
- While that's boiling like a bingo hall, make the ricotta sauce.
- In a medium bowl, mix ricotta, oil, parmesan, garlic, lemon rind and juice. Season with ¼ tsp of salt and a good pinch of pepper.
- In the last minute of the pasta cooking, save about ½ cup of the cooking water, then chuck the spinach in the pot with pasta. Stir well and push the leaves down in the water, cook for 1 minute. Drain pasta and spinach well.
- Return pasta and spinach to dry stockpot. Add the ricotta sauce and a splash of the saved cooking water, stir to evenly coat the pasta in the sauce. Add more cooking water if needed – you want a smooth and creamy sauce.
- Serve immediately with grated parmesan and a drizzle of extra virgin olive oil.

> *I love adding a good pinch of chilli flakes and squeezing some fresh lemon over. Deadly!*

# Spaghetti Napolitana for a Crowd

## Serves: 8 to 10

*A cheap and simple pasta meal that'll satisfy the hungriest of mobs. Add extra ingredients like sliced olives, salami, pancetta or mushrooms. When cooking the pasta, boil the kettle so you can top up the cooking water.*

2 onions
6 cloves garlic
⅓ cup olive oil
2 x 800g cans crushed tomatoes
2 x 500g pkts spaghetti *(or other long pasta)*
1 cup fresh basil leaves

## Method:
- Peel onions and garlic and finely chop.
- Heat oil in a large saucepan over low heat. Add onion and garlic and cook until onion is softened, about 10 to 12 minutes.
- Stir in tomatoes, half the basil and 1½ cups water, simmer for 35 to 40 minutes or until sauce has thickened and oil starts to come to top of sauce. Season well with salt and pepper.
- Meanwhile, cook spaghetti in a large stockpot of boiling, salted water until al dentè. *(The spaghetti should be tender but still have a little resistant bite in the centre.)*
- Drain spaghetti. *(Save about 1 cup of the cooking water.)* Return spaghetti to dry stockpot. Pour over half the tomato sauce and some of the reserved cooking water and return to a medium heat stirring about 1 to 2 minutes or until sauce coats the spaghetti well.

*Serve with remaining sauce and basil leaves.*

# Simple Spaghetti Marinara
**Serves: 4**

*Grab some marinara mix from the fish counter or fish monger and you'll have a simple cheap go-to meal to feed for when the mob turns up.*

4 cloves garlic
45g can anchovy fillets
2 tablespoons olive oil
2 x 400g can chopped tomatoes
¾ cup dry white wine *(or chicken stock)*
500g spaghetti *(or other long pasta)*
750g fresh marinara mix
½ cup chopped parsley

## Method:
- Peel and finely chop garlic. Drain anchovy fillets on paper towel.
- Heat oil in a large frypan over low to medium heat. Throw in garlic and anchovies, cook stirring until anchovies cook down to a soft paste and garlic is pale golden.
- Stir in tomatoes and wine *(or stock)* and bring to a boil, gently boil for about 20 minutes or until sauce is nice and thick. *(Once the seafood is added it will release a fair amount of liquid.)* Season well with salt and pepper.
- Meanwhile, cook spaghetti in a large stockpot of boiling, salted water until al dentè. Drain and return to stockpot.
- Add marinara mix to sauce and return to a boil, boil gently for 3 to 4 minutes or until seafood is cooked.
- Add marinara sauce and parsley to spaghetti in pot, mix well.
- Feed 'em like Mungo did!

*Serve with chilli flakes and lemon wedges if you like.*

# Fettuccine with Tuna

**Serves: 3 to 4**

*Feed the mob with this delicious, easy meal using pantry staples.*

1 small onion
2 garlic cloves
400g fettuccine *(or any other long pasta)*
¼ cup extra virgin olive oil
400g can crushed tomatoes
185g can tuna in olive oil
¼ cup chopped parsley

## Method:
• Peel onion and garlic and finely chop.
• Cook fettuccine in a large stockpot of boiling, salted water for 1 minute less than packet directions suggest. Drain fettuccine. *(Save about ½ cup of the cooking water.)*
• Meanwhile, heat oil in a large frypan over medium to high heat. Add onion and garlic, cook for 4 to 5 minutes or until onion is slightly softened, then chuck in tomatoes and ⅓ cup water. Simmer for 5 minutes. Drain tuna and add to sauce.
• Add pasta, sauce and reserved ½ cup cooking water back into stockpot. Cook over a medium heat tossing pasta until the sauce thickens and coats the pasta, about 1 to 2 minutes.
• Season with salt and pepper, toss through parsley.

*Seafood pasta is typically not served with parmesan, but you can if you want!*

# Hidden Vegie & Chicken Bake

**Serves: 6 to 8**

*Loaded with both hidden and visible vegetables. A comforting,
filling meal, the type of recipe that becomes a family favourite.*

300g chicken breast fillet
400g cauliflower
300g pasta (*penne, spiral, shells*)
2 tablespoons olive oil
3 handfuls spinach
40g butter
¼ cup plain flour
¾ cup milk
¾ cup chicken stock
2 cups grated tasty cheese

**Method:**
• Cut chicken into small, thin slices. Cut the cauliflower into
  florets.
• Cook pasta in a stockpot of boiling, salted water for about two
  thirds of the suggested cooking time on packet. Drain.
• Heat a large frypan over a medium to high heat, add chicken
  and cook about 5 to 6 minutes or until golden brown.
• Place cauliflower in a stockpot and cover with water, boil until
  tender. Stir in spinach, boil 1 minute. Remove from heat and
  drain off water. Puree cauli and spinach. (*I use a stick blender to
  do this.*)
• To make the sauce, melt butter in a medium saucepan over a
  low to medium heat. Sprinkle over flour and cook stirring for 1
  minute. Gradually whisk in milk and stock, whisking until sauce
  boils and thickens, gently boil for 1 minute. Remove from heat,
  stir in 1½ cups of the cheese.

- Add the cheese sauce to the cauli puree, season with salt and pepper.
- Stir in pasta and chicken and mix well. Tip the pasta mix into a large greased ovenproof dish, sprinkle over remaining grated cheese.
- Bake in oven at 180°C for 30 to 35 minutes or until cheese is melted and golden.

# Pappardelle Alfredo

**Serves: 4**

**CHEAP EATS**

*This simplest of pastas is rich and satisfying. Try adding chopped bacon or cooked chicken.*

375g egg pappardelle or fettucine
1 tablespoon butter
2 cloves garlic
300ml carton cream
1¼ cups finely grated parmesan
¼ cup finely chopped parsley

**Method:**
- Cook pappardelle in a stockpot of boiling, salted water until al dentè. Drain. *(Save about ½ cup of cooking water.)*
- Meanwhile, melt butter in medium frypan over a low heat. Add garlic and cook for 1 to 2 minutes or until pale golden. Add cream and bring to a boil. Lower heat, simmer for about 3 to 4 minutes or until cream is slightly reduced and coats the back of a spoon. Remove from heat and stir in parmesan. Season well with salt and pepper.
- Return pappardelle to stockpot, with sauce and parsley and toss together. Add a little reserved cooking water if sauce is too thick.

*Serve with extra parmesan sprinkled on top.*

# Bagettie & Meatballs with Sneaky Vegies

## Serves: 6
*Teach the kidlets how to make this pasta stunner – it's a tasty family meal packed with nutrients.*

1 onion
1 carrot
1 to 2 zucchini
300g pork sausages
500g beef mince
1 tablespoon dried oregano
½ cup finely grated parmesan
1 egg
3 cloves garlic
1 tablespoon olive oil
1 tablespoon tomato paste
1 teaspoon sugar
2 x 400g cans chopped tomatoes
500g spaghetti

## Method
- Peel onion and carrot and finely grate. Coarsely grate zucchini.
- Get the children to squeeze all the sausage meat out of the sausage skins into a large bowl, then add the mince.
- Throw in the grated onion, carrot, oregano, parmesan and egg, season well with salt and pepper and mix together with clean hands. Have the kids roll the meatball mix into walnut–sized balls and place them on a plate.
- While the kids are busy, make the sauce. Peel garlic and finely chop. Heat oil in a large saucepan. Add garlic and zucchini, cook for 5 minutes or until softened. Stir in tomato paste and sugar, cook for 1 minute. Add tomatoes, bring to a boil, simmer for 5 minutes. Remove from heat.

- If your children like zucchini then you can leave the sauce chunky. But if, like mine, they hate zucchini then remove pan from heat and blitz the sauce with a stick mixer.
- Heat oil in ya favourite large frypan, cook meatballs in batches until browned all over, then pop them into the sauce and simmer for 15 minutes or until meatballs are cooked through.
- Meanwhile, cook spaghetti in a stockpot of boiling, salted water until al dentè. Drain. Add meatballs and sauce to pot with spaghetti, toss and serve.

*Sprinkle with extra grated parmesan and a few torn basil leaves your child has picked. Lubly!*

# Knockout Noodles & Rice

Rice and noodles have a special place in many cultures and recipes across the globe. Even here in Australia we have a number of wild rice types that Indigenous people have been collecting for thousands of years. Below are just a few of my favourite ways to cook with these small yet important ingredients.

# Express Chow Mein

**Serves: 4**

*A quick and easy, cheap meal for a lunch snack or to feed the family. I have used the shelf fresh soba noodles, but you can use your favourite and follow packet directions for cooking.*

1 onion
3 stalks celery
¼ cup reduced sodium soy sauce
2 teaspoons minced garlic
1 tablespoon brown sugar
2 teaspoons crushed ginger
¼ teaspoon white pepper
2 x 180g pkts Japanese soba noodles
2 cups shredded cabbage
2 tablespoons olive oil

## Method:

- Peel onion and finely chop. Slice celery diagonally.
- Grab a small bowl and whisk together soy sauce, garlic, brown sugar, ginger and white pepper, set aside.
- Cook soba noodles in a stockpot of boiling water until noodles have loosened, about 1 to 2 minutes, drain well.
- Heat oil in a wok or large frypan over medium high heat. Chuck in onion and celery, cook stirring about 3 to 4 minutes or until slightly softened.
- Toss in cabbage, stir fry about 1 minute or until starting to wilt
- Add noodles and soy sauce mixture, stir fry until well combined and heated through, about 1 to 2 minutes.

# Beef Noodle Stir Fry

**Serves: 4**

*The easiest stir fry ever! And you can add in your favourite vegies or use a pack of fresh prepared vegies from the supermarket.*

250g sirloin steak
250g Swiss brown mushrooms
2 carrots
⅓ cup reduced sodium soy sauce
¼ cup oyster sauce
1 tablespoon brown sugar
1 tablespoon crushed ginger
1 teaspoon minced garlic
1 teaspoon sesame oil
200g packet Japanese udon noodles
2 tablespoons vegetable oil
200g broccoli florets

**Method:**
- Cut steak across the grain into thin slices. Slice mushrooms.
- Peel carrots and cut into 1cm pieces.
- Grab a small bowl and whisk together soy sauce, oyster sauce, brown sugar, ginger, garlic, sesame oil and ¼ teaspoon black pepper.
- Cook noodles according to packet directions. Drain well.
- Heat oil in a wok or large frypan over medium to high heat. Throw in beef and cook about 3 to 4 minutes or until browned. Remove beef from pan.
- Chuck mushrooms, broccoli and carrots into pan. Cook, stirring for 3 to 4 minutes or until slightly softened.
- Stir in noodles, beef and soy sauce mixture and cook until well combined and heated through, about 1 to 2 minutes. Lubly lah!

# Quick Creamy Miso Ramen

**Serves: 2**

*A cheeky, cheap, homemade, flavoursome ramen.*

2 spring onions
1 lemon
¼ cup extra virgin olive oil
1 tablespoon miso paste
⅓ cup finely grated parmesan
2 x 120g pkts ramen noodles *(use whatever flavour you like)*

## Method:

- Finely slice spring onions. Finely grate lemon rind, then juice lemons. *(You will need 2 tablespoons.)*
- Put a stockpot of water on the stove to boil.
- Meanwhile, throw the olive oil, miso paste, parmesan, lemon rind and lemon juice in a large frying pan over medium heat. Cook stirring until the parmesan and miso dissolve a little. *(Don't worry, it will look a little lumpy at this stage.)* Set aside.
- Cook the ramen noodle cakes in boiling water for 2 minutes or until tender. *(Keep seasoning sachets for later.)* Drain noodles reserving about ⅓ cup of the noodle cooking water.
- Throw the noodles and the reserved cooking water into the frypan with the sauce.
- Return to a medium heat, toss noodles in the sauce for 2 to 3 minutes or until the sauce has thickened and everything looks thick, shiny and luscious.
- Toss through the spring onions and a sprinkle of the seasoning sachet if you like.

*Serve with extra grated parmesan.*

# Singapore Curry Chicken Noodles

**Serves: 4**

*This has been a Koori favourite for years.*

350g chicken thigh fillets
2 tablespoons hoisin sauce
⅓ cup soy sauce
½ teaspoon cornflour
250g rice vermicelli noodles
2 red onions
4 cloves garlic
1 red capsicum
1 cup snow or snap peas
3 eggs
¼ cup vegetable oil
2 tablespoons dry sherry *(optional)*
2 teaspoons curry powder
1 teaspoons sugar

**Method:**
• Cut chicken into bite–size pieces. Place in a bowl with hoisin sauce, 1 tablespoon of the soy sauce and cornflour, mix well. Cover and refrigerate.
• Place noodles in a large heatproof bowl and cover with boiling water. Leave for 2 minutes, drain and rinse under cold running water. Drain.
• Peel onions and garlic and finely chop. Chop capsicum into bite–size pieces. Trim snow peas and slice.
• Whisk eggs together in a small bowl.
• Heat oil in a large wok or frypan over a high heat, add chicken.
• Stir fry until golden brown. Push chicken to one side of wok or pan, pour in whisked eggs. Allow to cook for a minute then break the egg up into pieces.

- Chuck in onions, garlic, capsicum and snow peas, stir fry for 1 minute.
- Pour in sherry, cook until sherry has evaporated. Stir in curry powder, sugar, remaining soy sauce and noodles.
- Toss noodles until they are well coated in sauce and heated through.

# Besties Broccoli & Cauli Rice
**Serves: 4**

1 red onion
1 red or green capsicum
200g shiitake mushrooms
160g baby spinach leaves
2 cups cauliflower and broccoli rice *(fresh or frozen)*
2 tablespoons garlic–infused olive oil
200g diced bacon

**Method:**
- Peel onion and finely chop. Chop capsicum and mushrooms into 1cm pieces.
- Shred spinach.
- Cook the cauliflower and broccoli rice according to packet directions.
- Heat oil in a large frypan over a medium heat. Throw in onion and bacon, cook stirring until onion is slightly softened.
- Add capsicum and mushrooms, cook for 3 minutes. Stir in cauli and broccoli rice and spinach and cook until heated through.

*Serve immediately or store in containers in the fridge.*

# Thai Chicken with Sweet Soy Noodles

**Serves: 2**

*A delicious Thai–inspired meal with a thick sauce and noodles, easily doubled.*

200g chicken thigh fillets
1 tablespoon oyster sauce
½ teaspoon ground white pepper
2 cloves garlic
½ bunch gai lan *(Chinese broccoli)*
1 tablespoon cornflour
¼ cup vegetable oil
440g pkt wok–ready rice noodles *(or fresh rice noodles)*
1 tablespoon kecap manis
1 cup chicken stock
2 tablespoons fish sauce

**Method:**
- Thinly slice chicken, mix with oyster sauce and ½ teaspoon of the white pepper.
- Peel garlic and finely chop. Cut gai lan leaves and stalks diagonally into thin slices.
- Mix cornflour with 2 tablespoons water until smooth.
- Heat 1 tablespoon of the oil in a wok or large frying pan over high heat.

**TIP**
For a spicy tangy kick, mix together 1 sliced long red chilli and ¼ cup white vinegar. Spoon over a little before serving.

- Toss in the rice noodles, spread them out and allow to cook for a few seconds. Stir, then cook undisturbed for 30 seconds. Once noodles start to char at edges, add 2 teaspoons of the kecap manis and stir fry for 30 seconds. Place noodles in a serving dish.
- In the same frypan, heat remaining oil over high heat. Chuck in the chicken and stir fry for 3 to 4 minutes or until cooked through and starting to char.
- Throw in the garlic and gai lan, stir fry for 30 seconds.
- Pour in chicken stock, fish sauce, remaining kecap manis and white pepper. Gradually pour in the cornflour mixture, stirring until sauce boils and thickens, simmer for 1 minute until thick and glossy.
- Spoon chicken and sauce over top of noodles.

*Sprinkle with chilli powder. Deadly as!*

# Rach's Special Devon Fried Rice

**Serves: 8**

*A deadly fried rice with a devon twist. Fills up to 4
rectangular takeaway containers and can be frozen and
then reheated when needed.*

2 cups long grain or jasmine rice
500g devon roll *(coz devon is the answer to everything)*
500g mixed fresh vegies
2 teaspoons vegetable oil
8 eggs
2 to 3 tablespoons soy sauce

## Method *(to my Madness):*

- Wash your rice before cooking! Then cook rice according to
  packet directions or use a rice cooker *(see page 239)*. Place on a
  tray in fridge to cool.
- Cut devon and vegies into 1 to 2cm pieces.
- Heat oil in a large non–stick wok or frypan over medium heat.
- Whisk eggs together and pour into wok swirling over base to
  form an omelette. Cook for 2 minutes or until set. Place on a
  chopping board to cool slightly. Cut into thin short strips.
- Add devon to wok, stir fry for 4 minutes or until light golden.
  Chuck in mixed vegies and stir fry for 1 minute.
- Add rice and cook for 3
  to 4 minutes, stirring only
  occasionally so that rice goes
  nice and crisp on the base.
- Toss through egg and soy sauce,
  stir fry until heated through.

*Serve in bowls sprinkled with
sesame seeds & chopped shallots.
Madfeedz!*

**TIP**

Use a mix of any
vegetables you
like in this: celery,
carrots, peas, beans,
zucchini, broccoli,
corn.

# Kung Pao Chicken Rice

**Serves: 4**

*Crunch and spice come together in this fragrant chicken dinner. If you want to cook your own rice use 1 cup of long grain rice.*

600g chicken thigh fillets
2 red capsicums
5 spring onions
2 long fresh red chillies
2 x 250g pkts microwave long grain white rice
2 tablespoons vegetable oil
½ cup salted peanuts
145g pkt Lee Kum Kee ready sauce for Kung Pao Chicken
1 tablespoon crushed ginger

**Method:**
- Cut chicken into 3cm pieces. Chop capsicums into 2cm pieces.
- Thinly slice spring onions and red chillies.
- Cook rice according to packet directions.
- Heat oil in a large frypan over high heat.
- Throw in the chicken in two batches and cook for 6 to 7 minutes or until browned. Remove from pan.
- Chuck capsicum, chillies and peanuts into the frypan. Cook, stirring over medium heat for 3 minutes or until capsicum is slightly softened.
- Return chicken to the pan. Add kung pao sauce, ginger, ⅓ cup water, rice and half the spring onions. Cook stirring occasionally for 5 to 6 minutes or until heated through.
- Sprinkle over remaining spring onions to serve.

# One Pot Chicken & Lemon Rice
**Serves: 5**

*A deadly meal where the rice is the hero! Chicken and lemon–flavoured rice. Lubly lah!*

1 onion
4 cloves garlic
2 lemons
5 chicken thigh cutlets *(skin on)*
1½ tablespoons dried oregano leaves
1 tablespoon olive oil
1 cup long grain white rice
1½ cups chicken stock

**Method:**
- Peel onion and garlic and finely chop. Finely grate the rind from lemons, then juice lemons. *(You will need ⅓ cup.)*
- Combine the chicken with lemon rind and juice, garlic, half the oregano and ½ teaspoon salt in a large zip lock bag and refrigerate for at least 20 minutes but preferably a few hours.
- Remove chicken from marinade, reserve marinade.
- Heat oil in a heavy based, flameproof, ovenproof pot over medium to high heat. *(A French–style, enamelled cast iron casserole pot is ideal for this.)*
- Chuck the chicken in the pot, skin side down, cook until golden brown on both sides. Remove from pan. Pour off excess fat.
- Chuck in the onion, cook for 3 minutes or until slightly softened.

- Add remaining oregano, rice, stock, ¾ cup water, ½ teaspoon salt, ¼ teaspoon pepper and reserved marinade. Bring to a boil, remove from heat.
- Arrange the chicken over top of rice. Cover with lid. Cook in oven at 180°C for 35 minutes. Remove the lid and cook a further 10 minutes, or until all the liquid is absorbed and chicken is cooked through.
- Remove from oven and set aside for 5 to 10 minutes before serving.

*Serve with extra grated lemon rind or chopped parsley sprinkled over.*

*This dish tastes even better if you marinate the chicken overnight.*

# Cakes & Extra Goodies

Cakes and other sweet treats are not only delicious to eat but the kids love to get involved as well. That's where I started my kitchen journey, making cakes while the family watched TV after dinner.

# Chocolate Chip Cookies
**Makes: 12**

*Soft and gooey on the inside – absolutely perfect!*

125g butter
½ cup white sugar
¾ cup brown sugar, well packed
½ teaspoon salt
1 egg
1 teaspoon vanilla extract
1¼ cups plain flour
½ teaspoon bicarb soda
⅔ cup milk choc bits
⅔ cup dark choc bits

## Method:
- Line two baking trays with baking paper. Melt butter in a small saucepan over a low heat.
- Chuck both sugars, salt and butter into a large bowl and whisk together to make a smooth paste. Add egg and vanilla, whisk until well combined.
- Mix together flour and bicarb soda then add to sugar mixture, stirring to just bring mixture together. *(Don't overmix.)*
- Sprinkle over choc bits and mix through dough. Chill in fridge for at least 30 minutes.
- Use a small ice cream scoop to scoop the dough out onto prepared trays, rounded side up, leave at least 10cm of space between cookies and 5cm space from edges of tray *(so the cookies can spread).*
- Cook in oven at 180°C for 12 to 15 minutes, or until the edges have only just started to brown. Cool completely on trays. Lubly!

# Rich Hot Chocolate Fudge Sauce
**Makes: 1 cup**

*A thick, rich sauce perfect served warm over ice cream or brownies.*

150g dark chocolate
½ cup cream
2 tablespoons brown sugar
½ teaspoon vanilla essence

## Method:
- Chop chocolate into small pieces.
- Throw chocolate, cream, brown sugar and vanilla essence into a small saucepan.
- Stir over low to medium heat until chocolate melts and ingredients are well combined.
- Remove from heat and serve warm or at room temperature. *(The sauce will thicken as it cools.)* Store in an airtight container in the fridge for up to 1 week.

# Easy Milo Balls

**Makes: 20**

*These deadly easy Milo balls are sure to be a hit with the kidlets.*

250g pkt plain sweet biscuits *(like Marie or Milk Arrowroot)*
395g can sweetened condensed milk
1 cup desiccated coconut
⅓ cup Milo powder
Extra desiccated coconut, to coat

## Method:

- Crush the biscuits in a food processor until they resemble fine breadcrumbs.
- Place into a large bowl, add the condensed milk, coconut and Milo and mix well.
- Get the kidlets to help roll mixture into heaped teaspoon–size balls, then coat in extra coconut.
- Store in the fridge in an airtight container for up to 5 days *(or freeze)*.

# A Basic Vanilla Cake

**Serves: 12**

*This made–from–scratch vanilla cake is light and full of buttery vanilla flavour. Change it up and add other flavourings like orange or lemon rind or a couple of handfuls of choc bits, sultanas or currants.*

185g butter, softened
1 cup caster sugar
1 teaspoon vanilla essence
3 large eggs
2 cups self raising flour
¼ cup milk

## Method:

- Crank the oven up to 180°C and grease a deep 20cm round cake pan well. *(You can line the base with baking paper to make it easier to remove cake.)*
- In a large bowl, beat the butter, sugar and vanilla together in an electric mixer until light and creamy.
- Crack the eggs in one at a time and beat well after each addition. Remove bowl from mixer.
- Sift over flour alternating with the milk, adding about a third at a time. Stir lightly until all ingredients are combined. *(Don't overmix!)*
- Spoon mixture into prepared pan and cook in oven for 50 to 55 minutes or until a skewer inserted in the centre of cake comes out clean.
- Cool cake in pan for 5 to 10 minutes, then turn out onto a wire rack to cool.

*Cake can be iced or dusted with icing sugar.*

# JENNNNAAAYY'S No Bake Choc Slice

**Serves: 6**

*Hello, darlings! This was inspired by a favourite TikToker of mine. It's quick, simple and delicious, and you can get the kids involved.*

250g pkt Choc Ripple biscuits
200g block chocolate (*milk or dark*)
395g can sweetened condensed milk
Chocolates of choice for topping (*I used Caramilk Twirl Bites for mine*)

**Method:**
- Line an 18cm x 28cm rectangular slice pan with baking paper.
- Crush up biscuits in a food processor or punch or crush them using your hands to get some stress out. Tip into a large bowl.
- Break up chocolate into pieces and chuck into a microwave-safe bowl. Pour in the condensed milk and microwave for about 1 minute, stir well and microwave again for another 30 seconds to 1 minute or until chocolate is melted when stirred. (*Don't overcook!*)
- Tip melted chocolate mixture into the crushed biscuits and give 'em a stirring until well combined. Pour into prepared pan and smooth over top.
- Place on toppings of choice and push into the top of the slice.
- Throw it in the fridge and leave to firm up for about 2 hours.
- Cut up like Souths cut up Canterbury in 2014 and enjoy it as much as I did. GGTSS! SSTID!

# Triple Layer Supermarket Mud Cake

**Serves: 6 or more**

*With this one let your imagination run wild. It's best to start the day before to allow for lots of chilling as it makes it easier.*

3 x supermarket mud cakes *(use the same flavour or mix it up)*
2 x 400g tubs creamy deluxe frosting *(or make your own)*
Aussie favourite biscuits and chocolates, to decorate

**Method:**
• Freeze cakes at least one day before using.
• Remove from freezer and trim the icing off to ensure the top is as level as possible. Repeat this process for all three layers. Set icing aside until thawed.
• Process icing in a food processor or beat with electric beaters until smooth. *(If mixture is too thick, add a little water.)*
• The icing glaze is one of the best parts and helps the cake layers stick together.
• Stack the three cakes by spreading a layer of icing between each cake.
• Now place your assembled cake on a board or serving plate and use some of the prepared frosting and an icing spatula to cover cake all over top and side with a layer of frosting. *(Don't worry too much about how it looks at this point.)* Place in the fridge for about 30 minutes or until firm.
• Spread another layer of frosting over top and side of cakes, smoothing with the icing spatula.
• Use a smaller kitchen knife to fluff up the icing on the top, or if you want a smooth top, use the icing spatula.
• Decorate the top with whatever biscuits or chocolates you like!

# Chocolate Brownie Cake

**Serves: 6 to 8**

 *Get kids cooking at the weekend by baking this yummy brownie cake – much better than shop bought.*

100g butter
½ cup caster sugar
⅓ cup brown sugar, well packed
125g milk or dark chocolate
1 tablespoon golden syrup
2 eggs
1 teaspoon vanilla extract
¾ cup plain flour
½ teaspoon baking powder
2 tablespoon cocoa powder

**Method:**
• Crank that oven up to 180°C. Grease and line a 20cm square cake pan with baking paper
• Chuck the butter, sugars, chocolate and golden syrup into a medium saucepan and stir gently over a low heat until smooth and lump–free. Remove from heat, cool until warm.
• Break eggs into a large bowl and whisk with a fork until light and frothy. Add eggs to chocolate mixture with vanilla, flour, baking powder and cocoa powder and whisk together.
• Pour brownie mixture into prepared cake pan. Place on middle shelf of oven. Cook for 25 to 30 minutes or until brownie is firm not wobbly in centre.
• Remove and allow to cool completely before cutting into pieces.

*Serve with cream or ice cream and plenty of fresh fruit.*

# Homemade Easy Lamingtons
**Serves: 12**

*An Australian classic made easy at home, delicious sponge cake dipped in chocolate and covered in coconut.*

½ cup plain flour

¼ cup cornflour

½ teaspoon baking powder

2 tablespoons milk

1 tablespoon butter

3 large eggs

¼ cup caster sugar

2 cups desiccated or shredded coconut

## Chocolate icing

½ cup cocoa powder

2 cups icing sugar

2 tablespoons unsalted butter

½ cup milk

## Method:
- Grease and line a 20cm square cake pan with baking paper, leaving 3cm of paper to overhang pan edges.
- Sift flour, cornflour and baking powder twice into a large mixing bowl.
- Pour milk and butter into a small saucepan and heat gently until butter is melted. Cool slightly.
- Meanwhile, place eggs in bowl of an electric mixer, beat until thick and foamy. Add sugar, one tablespoon at a time beating until very thick and pale in colour *(about 5 to 8 minutes)*.
- Meanwhile, crank oven up to 180°C.

- Sift flour mixture over top of egg mixture and pour butter mixture in around the inside of bowl. Gently fold ingredients until just combined. *(Don't overmix!)*
- Pour mixture into prepared pan. Cook in oven for 20 to 22 minutes or until the cake gently springs back when lightly touched on top. Remove from oven, leave to cool for 5 minutes, then lift cake from pan using baking paper sides. Place on a wire rack on the paper until completely cool.
- To make chocolate icing, sift cocoa powder and icing sugar together into a large bowl. Melt butter and milk together in a small saucepan. Add to cocoa mixture, stir until icing is smooth.
- Cut sponge cake into 12 pieces. Carefully and quickly dip each piece of cake into chocolate icing, let the excess icing drip off, then coat each piece in coconut. Transfer to a cake rack to dry.
- Repeat with remaining cake squares. Lubly lah!

# Chocolate Crackles

**Makes: 20**

*These 60s party classics were a crackle back then and are still a cracking treat now.*

250g block copha
4 cups Rice Bubbles
1 cup icing sugar
½ cup cocoa powder
1 cup desiccated coconut

## Method:

• Line 2 x 12 cup patty cake trays with 20 paper cases.
• Melt copha in a small saucepan over a very low heat until just melted. Cool slightly.
• Mix Rice Bubbles, icing sugar, cocoa powder and coconut in a large bowl.
• Pour over the melted copha and stir until all ingredients are well combined.
• Spoon crackle mix evenly into the prepared paper cases.
• Place in fridge for at least 1 hour or until firm.

*Store in an airtight container in the fridge for up to 5 days.*

# Anzac Biscuits

**Makes: 18**

 *These date back to 1915. I like to think my great-grandfather ate them in France. Lest we forget.*

1 cup quick oats
1 cup sweetened coconut flakes
1 cup plain flour
1 cup white sugar
125g butter
2 tablespoons golden syrup
1 teaspoons bicarb soda
2 tablespoons boiling water

## Method:
- Fire up the oven to 180°C. Line 2 x baking trays with baking paper.
- Throw oats, coconut, flour and sugar in a large bowl.
- In a medium saucepan, melt butter and golden syrup over a medium heat. Remove from heat.
- Mix bicarb soda with boiling water, add to butter mixture. *(It will bubble up.)*
- Pour the butter mixture into the dry ingredients and mix well.
- Roll tablespoonsful of mixture into balls, place on the baking paper about 5cm apart. *(They do spread!)*
- Flatten cookies with your hand or a fork. Cook in oven for 12 to 15 minutes or until golden brown.
- Cool on trays until warm, then move to a wire rack to cool completely. Lubly!

TIP

You can use also use traditional rolled oats and desiccated coconut instead of flakes.

# Chocolate Caramel Slice

**Makes: 16 slices**

*I couldn't leave this one out.*

### Base
1 cup plain flour
½ cup brown sugar, well packed
½ cup desiccated coconut
125g butter

### Caramel Filling
⅓ cup golden syrup
2 x 395g cans sweetened condensed milk
Extra 125g butter

### Topping
200g milk or dark chocolate
3 teaspoons vegetable oil *(or coconut oil)*

### Method:
- Grease and line an 18cm x 28cm rectangular slice pan with baking paper.
- Crank oven up to 180°C. Melt butter in a small saucepan over a low heat.
- To make the base, mix together flour, brown sugar and coconut. Pour in melted butter and mix until well combined.
- Press the mixture firmly into the base of prepared pan, smooth over surface with back of a spoon. Cook in oven for 15 minutes or until light golden.
- Meanwhile, make filling, place golden syrup, condensed milk and extra butter into a small saucepan over a very low heat. Stir continuously for 10 to 12 minutes or until the caramel has thickened and darkened slightly.

- Pour the caramel over the cooked base and cook in the oven for a further 15 to 20 minutes or until golden and firm when pan is wobbled.
- Remove from the oven and set aside until cool. Place in the fridge to cool completely.
- To make topping, break chocolate into pieces, place chocolate and vegetable oil in a microwave–proof bowl and microwave on 50 per cent power for 3 to 4 minutes or until just melted, stirring every 30 seconds with a dry metal spoon.
- Spread the melted chocolate over the cooled caramel layer. Leave at room temperature to set. Cut into slices.

*Store in an airtight container for up to 5 days.*

# The Best Damn Fairy Bread

**Serves:4**

 *Another retro party classic, served with red cordial. The kids will be buzzing like it's pay day.*

4 slices white bread
50g butter, softened
½ cup 100's and 1000's Sprinkles

**Method:**
- Cut the the crusts from each slice of bread. Gently spread each slice with butter.
- Drown bread with sprinkles, patting down gently so they stick. Tipping off excess.
- Slice each piece of Fairy Bread into triangles and serve. Awwww deadly!

# After-School Snacks

These deadly after-school snacks will keep the rugrats at bay until dinner. Get them involved in helping to make their own snacks with these quick, easy recipes.

# Easy Fruit Salad with Yoghurt
**Serves: 6 to 8**

*A tasty after–school treat.*

4 mandarins

2 apples

2 cups strawberries

1 cup red grapes

½ cup natural yoghurt

1 tablespoon honey

**Method:**
- Peel the mandarins and separate into segments, cut into pieces.
- Remove and discard core from apples, cut into 1.5cm pieces.
- Hull strawberries and cut into halves or quarters. Cut grapes in half lengthways.
- Combine all the prepared fruit in a bowl.
- In a small bowl, mix together yoghurt and honey.
- Pour the yoghurt mixture over the fruit and mix together.

TIP

If making ahead, add yoghurt just before serving.

# Hummus with Carrots & Celery

**Serves: 4**

*CHEAP EATS*

*A quick and easy tasty snack.*

2 cloves garlic
400g can chickpeas
¼ cup extra virgin olive oil
1½ tablespoons tahini
Juice of 1 lemon
1 tablespoon finely chopped coriander leaves *(optional)*
2 large carrots
4 stalks celery
2 wholemeal pita breads

**Method:**

- Peel garlic and roughly chop. Drain chickpeas and rinse under cold running water, drain well.
- Heat the oil in a small frypan over a low to medium heat, add the garlic, and cook stirring for 2 to 3 minutes or until very pale golden.
- Remove from the heat, cool slightly.
- Place the chickpeas, tahini, lemon juice, garlic and oil in a food processor and process until smooth, adding a little water to loosen the mixture.
- Season to taste with salt and stir through coriander *(if using)*. Spoon into a bowl, cover and refrigerate until ready to serve.
- Peel carrots and cut carrots and celery into thin sticks.

*Serve hummus with carrot and celery sticks and torn–up pita bread.*

# Cheese & Vegemite Scrolls

**Makes: 10**

*Fantastic for after school or perfect for the lunchbox. Use your kids' favourite cheese.*

50g butter
3 cups self raising flour
1 to 1½ cups milk
1 to 2 tablespoons vegemite
1½ cups shredded cheese

**Method:**
- Crank the oven up to 220°C. Grease and line a large baking tray with baking paper.
- Cut butter into 1cm pieces.
- Sift flour and pinch of salt into a large bowl. Toss in butter and rub in with your fingertips until mixture resembles fine breadcrumbs.
- Stir in enough milk to make a soft dough.
- Knead gently on a lightly floured benchtop. Roll out to a rectangle shape measuring about 25cm x 40cm.
- Spread vegemite over the dough using a blunt knife. Sprinkle over 1 cup of the cheese.
- Roll up the dough starting from the long side to form a long roll.
- Cut roll into 10 x 4cm thick slices. Place slices close together, cut side up on prepared tray.
- Sprinkle the remaining cheese over the top of slices. Cook in oven for 15 to 20 minutes or until golden brown.

# Ham & Corn Muffins

**Serves: 12**

*Like a meal in a muffin!*

125g butter
¾ cup corn kernels *(canned or fresh)*
2 cups self raising flour
½ cup shredded tasty cheese
¾ cup chopped ham
1 tablespoon chopped chives
1 cup milk
1 egg

**Method:**
• Crank the oven to 190°C. Grease a 12 hole muffin pan with cooking oil spray.
• Melt butter in a small saucepan over low heat. Set aside.
• Sift the flour into a large bowl. Add cheese, ham, corn and chives, mix well.
• Whisk milk and egg together with a fork, add to flour mixture with melted butter and gently fold through with a metal spoon until just combined.
• Divide the mixture between the muffin holes and cook in oven for 15 to 20 minutes or until golden.
• Leave to cool in the pan for 5 to 10 minutes, then place muffins on a wire rack to cool completely.

# Berry Banana Smoothie

**Serves: 2**

*A delicious after–school drink when it's been a hot day at school.*

1 large banana
2½ cups frozen berries *(use your favourites)*
1¼ cups almond milk *(or oat, soy or cow's milk)*
½ cup Greek–style yoghurt

**Method:**
- Break banana into pieces, place in blender with all other ingredients and blitz until thick and smooth.
- Divide between 2 cups, enjoy!

# Strawberry Watermelon Icies

**Makes: 4**

 *Get the kids in the kitchen to help make these delicious popsicles.*

2 cups watermelon flesh
2 teaspoons lemon juice *(optional)*
10 strawberries

**Method:**
- Chuck watermelon, lemon juice *(if using)* and strawberries into a blender. Blitz until smooth.
- Pour into ice pop moulds and freeze for at least 6 hours.

# Homemade Muesli Bars

**Makes: 16**

*Keep the kidlets happy with these homemade muesli bars – soft and chewy with just the right amount of crunch.*

½ cup coconut oil
½ cup honey
½ cup peanut butter or any nut butter
¼ teaspoon ground cinnamon
1 teaspoon vanilla extract
⅔ cup brown sugar
1⅔ cups rolled oats
½ cup desiccated coconut
1¼ cups trail mix *(mix of nuts, seeds and dried fruit)*
⅓ cup plain flour
1 cup puffed rice
½ cup milk or dark choc bits

## Method:
• Grease and line a 20cm x 28cm rectangular slice pan with baking paper.
• Chuck the coconut oil, honey and peanut butter into a microwave-proof bowl.
• Heat in 30 second bursts *(stirring well after each 30 seconds)* until just melted.
• Add cinnamon, vanilla and brown sugar, mix well.
• Throw rolled oats, coconut, trail mix, flour and puffed rice into a large bowl. Add the honey mixture and mix all ingredients together. Stir through choc bits.
• Tip the mixture into prepared tray and press down firmly and evenly.
• Cook in oven at 160°C for 25 to 30 minutes or until just golden. Allow to cool completely in pan, then cut into slices.

# Toasted Muesli with Yoghurt

**Makes: about 4 cups**

*You can change this up by using different nuts and dried fruits.*

12 dried apricots
1 cup raw pecans
2 tablespoons butter
2 cups old–fashioned rolled oats
¾ cup raisins
2 tablespoons honey
½ teaspoon ground cinnamon

**Method:**
- Grease and line a large baking tray with baking paper. Chuck oven onto 200°C.
- Chop apricots into quarters. Roughly chop pecans.
- Melt butter in a small saucepan over low heat.
- Chuck oats, apricots, pecans and raisins in a medium bowl.
- Whisk together melted butter, honey and cinnamon in a small bowl.
- Pour over the oat mixture and stir well to coat.
- Pour muesli onto prepared baking sheet and spread into a single layer.
- Cook in oven for 5 minutes, stir and cook for 5 more minutes or until golden and crisp, watching it closely to make sure that it does not get too dark. Remove from oven and cool completely.
- Store in an airtight container.

*Serve as a crunchy snack or with yoghurt and fresh berries.*

# Chocolate Chip Muffins

**Makes: 12**

*These are a sure way to keep the kids happy and quiet.*

¾ cup milk
⅓ cup vegetable oil
1 egg
2 cups plain flour
½ cup white sugar
3 teaspoons baking powder
¾ cup mini choc bits
Extra ¼ cup white sugar
2 tablespoons brown sugar, well packed

**Method:**
- Crank oven up to 200°C. Line a standard 12 cup muffin pan with paper cases.
- Whisk milk, oil and egg together in a small bowl.
- Chuck flour, ½ cup sugar, baking powder and choc bits into a large bowl and mix well. Make a well in centre and gradually pour in milk mixture, stirring gently until dry ingredients are moistened. *(The batter will be lumpy.)*
- Spoon mixture into muffin cases to ⅔ full. Mix together extra white sugar and brown sugar and sprinkle over tops of muffins.
- Cook in oven for 20 to 25 minutes or until a skewer inserted in the centre of muffin comes out clean. Remove from oven and cool in pan for 5 minutes, then place on a wire rack. Serve warm.

# Banana Bread

**Serves: 10**

*For the ultimate treat, serve this moist banana bread fresh out of the oven with creamy butter.*

50g butter, melted, cooled
2 overripe medium bananas
2 eggs
1¾ cups self raising flour
¼ cup plain flour
1 teaspoon ground cinnamon
⅔ cup brown sugar, firmly packed
½ cup milk

## Method:

- Crank that oven up to 180°C. Grease and line an 11cm x 21cm loaf pan with baking paper, allowing paper to overhang edges slightly.
- Melt butter in a small saucepan over a low heat. Cool slightly.
- Mash bananas, set aside. Whisk eggs together with a fork in a small bowl.
- Sift flours and cinnamon into a large bowl. Stir in the sugar and make a well in the centre.
- Add in milk, melted butter, bananas and eggs, stir well.
- Pour banana mixture into flour mixture and stir until all ingredients are just combined. *(Don't overmix!)* Spoon mixture into prepared pan and smooth the surface.
- Cook in oven for 45 to 50 minutes or until a skewer inserted into the centre of cake comes out clean. Remove from oven and cool in pan for 5 minutes, then place onto a wire rack to cool completely. Cut into slices to serve.

# Honey Hotcakes
**Makes: 15**

*These protein rich hotcakes will satisfy hungry tummies after a day at school.*

200g tub cottage cheese
200g tub Greek yoghurt
3 eggs
½ cup milk *(or soy, almond or oat)*
2 tablespoons honey
½ cup wholemeal plain flour
¾ cup self raising flour
1 tablespoon butter

**Method:**
• Whisk together cottage cheese, yoghurt, eggs, milk and honey in a large bowl.
• Chuck in flours and whisk until combined.
• Melt about a teaspoon of the butter over base of ya frypan over medium heat. Pour ¼ cup batter into pan. Cook hotcake for 2 to 3 minutes or until bubbles form on surface and base is golden brown.
• Turn over and cook for about 1 to 2 minutes or until golden brown on both sides. Repeat with remaining batter, adding extra butter as you need it.

*Serve with sliced strawberries and extra honey.*

# Pita Gozleme

**Makes: 4**

*You can make these without spinach if the kids aren't fans.*

1 tablespoon olive oil
250g lamb or beef mince
1 teaspoon minced garlic
1 teaspoon ground cumin
400g can chopped tomatoes
100g frozen chopped spinach
100g feta cheese
1 cup shredded tasty cheese
420g pkt *(4)* pita bread pockets

## Method:

- Heat oil in ya large frypan over high heat. Cook mince for 4 to 5 minutes or until browned, stirring to break up mince.
- Stir in garlic and cumin, cook for 1 minute. Add tomatoes and spinach, gently boil for 15 minutes or until mixture is nice and thick. Remove from heat and cool.
- To make gozleme, split pita breads partly open up and spoon filling over base of bread. Top with crumbled feta and a sprinkle over shredded cheese. Fold top of bread back over filling to cover.
- Cook in a sandwich press or on an oven tray at 180°C until golden and crisp.

*Serve with lemon wedges for the full gozleme experience!*

# The Basics

Sounds simple enough and it is! Here are some helpful recipes and tips that'll guide you along the way and add to the adventure of creating your own madfeedz!

# Perfect Scrambled Eggs

**Serves: 1**

*Learn how to make perfect scrambled eggs with this easy recipe.*
*A quick breakfast packed with protein.*

2 large eggs
½ cup full cream milk
2 teaspoons butter

## Method:

- Lightly whisk eggs, milk and a pinch of salt together until well combined.
- Heat a small non–stick frying pan over a low to medium heat. Add butter and heat until melted. *(Don't let the butter brown.)*
- Pour in egg mixture, allow egg to cook without stirring for 20 seconds. Stir with a wooden spoon, lifting and folding over from the bottom of the pan.
- Cook without stirring for another 10 seconds, then stir and fold again.
- Repeat until the eggs are softly set and slightly runny in places. Remove from the heat and leave for a moment to finish cooking.
- Give a final stir and serve the velvety scramble immediately.

## GETTING THE BEST RESULTS

Always use a non–stick pan with a wooden spoon for best results and easy cleaning. Don't overstir, you are folding the eggs rather than scrambling. The eggs should have a soft curd–like texture. It's best not to cook too many eggs in one go (*no more than 4 eggs in a good sized frypan*) or the eggs won't cook as well. For larger numbers, cook in two pans rather than one.

# Classic Garlic Bread

**Serves: 6 to 8**

*A quick and simple snack for when the mob drop in on their way to the knockout.*

3 cloves garlic
125g unsalted butter
¼ cup extra virgin olive oil
½ cup finely chopped parsley leaves
1 baguette or bread stick
½ cup grated parmesan

## Method:
- Peel garlic and crush.
- Crank the oven up to 220°C. Place butter and oil in a small saucepan over medium heat.
- Throw in the garlic and parsley and cook, stirring occasionally, until butter is just melted, remove from heat.
- Slice bread in half lengthwise, then place on a baking tray and brush cut sides with butter mixture.
- Slice crosswise 3cm thick, without cutting all the way through. Season with salt and top with parmesan. Cook in oven for 10 to 15 minutes or until golden. Lubly lah!

# Cheap Cheesy Pasta

**Serves: 4 to 6**

*A real cheap and easy meal the kids can help make. Use your favourite pasta.*

500g penne pasta
500g jar cream cheese spread

**Method:**
- Cook pasta in a stockpot of boiling, salted water for 10 minutes or until pasta is just cooked, not soft. *(It should still have some bite to it.)*
- Drain well. Return pasta to pot.
- Spoon the cheese spread into pot with the pasta, stirring until the pasta is well coated.
- Divide between required numbers in the mob. Leftovers can be saved for lunch.

**TIP**
Use the Bold flavoured cream cheese spread for an extra cheesy flavour.

# Basic Pizza Dough
**Makes: 1**

*A simple way to make your own pizza from scratch.*

7g sachet dried yeast *(or 2 teaspoons active dried yeast)*
½ teaspoon caster sugar
1½ cups bread or pizza flour
½ teaspoon salt
1 tablespoon extra virgin olive oil

**Method:**
- Mix together yeast, sugar and ¾ cup warm water in a small jug. Stand for 10 to 15 minutes or until mixture starts to form bubbles on top.
- Mix together flour and salt in a large bowl. Make a well in the centre. Add in the yeast mixture and oil and stir until mixture forms a dough.
- Turn dough out onto a lightly floured benchtop. Knead, for 5 minutes or until smooth and elastic, adding more flour if needed. *(You can also do this in a stand mixer with a dough attachment.)*
- Place dough in a large, oiled bowl. Cover and set aside in a warm place for 1 hour or until doubled in size.
- Punch down dough. Knead for 20 seconds or until smooth. Roll out to a 23cm x 30cm rectangular pizza base. Place on a large greased baking tray.
- Crank up the oven to 240°C.
- Spread tomato paste on pizza base and add your favourite toppings and cheese. Cook in the oven for 10 to 12 minutes or until the base of pizza is golden brown and crisp.

# Classic Potato Mash

**Serves: 4 to 6**

A much–loved family favourite.

1kg potatoes
1 onion
2 tablespoons butter
½ cup warm milk
Extra butter, to serve

## Method:

• Peel and chop potatoes into 4cm pieces.
• Peel and chop onion into 1cm pieces.
• Chuck potatoes in a large saucepan and cover with water. Gently boil for 20 to 25 minutes or until potatoes are really tender. Drain.
• Return potatoes to pan with chopped onion, cook, stirring over low heat for 2 to 3 minutes or until dry. Remove from heat.
• Using a potato masher, mash until potato is smooth. Gradually mash in the butter and milk.
• Season with salt and white pepper. Top with extra butter.

*Use a good mashing potato. Sebago, spunta and desiree potatoes all make great mash.*

# Homemade Baked Beans

**Makes: 8 cups**

*Store a portion of these nutritious baked beans in the fridge to create delicious breakfasts and dinners in minutes.*

500g dried great northern or cannellini beans
2 large onions
3 garlic cloves
2 tablespoons olive oil
1 tablespoon chopped fresh thyme leaves
800g can diced tomatoes
1 litre chicken stock
1kg smoked ham hock

**Method**
• Place beans in a large bowl. Cover with cold water.
• Set aside for 8 hours or overnight to soak. Rinse well under running water. Drain.
• Peel onions and garlic and finely chop.
• Bung the oven on to 160°C.
• Heat oil in a large flameproof, ovenproof dish over a medium heat.
• Add onions, cook stirring occasionally, for 6 to 8 minutes or until softened.
• Add garlic and thyme. Cook for 2 minutes or until light golden.
• Chuck in tomatoes, stock, drained beans and ham hock. Cover with lid and bring to a boil. Remove from heat and carefully transfer to the oven.
• Cook in the oven for 3 hours, stirring occasionally, until beans are just tender. Cool until warm. Season with pepper.
• Transfer ham bone to a chopping board. Remove and discard rind, bone and fat. Shred ham and add back into pot, mix well.
• Serve warm or refrigerate until ready to use.

# White Sauce

**Makes: 2½ cups**

*The perfect sauce for corned beef or lasagne. Here's a simple and easy way to do it that tastes better than the packet sauce from the supermarket and is made from pantry staples. This recipe is easily doubled.*

2½ cups of milk
50g butter
⅓ cup plain flour

**Method:**
- Heat milk in a saucepan until warm, set aside.
- Melt butter in another medium saucepan over a low heat. Sprinkle over flour stirring until smooth and bubbling. Cook stirring for 1 minute.
- Gradually whisk in the hot milk and continue whisking over a medium heat until sauce is gently bubbling and thickened. Boil gently for 1 to 2 minutes, stirring.
- Season with salt and pepper.

*To make a cheese sauce, stir in ½ cup grated tasty cheese and ½ cup grated parmesan once pan is removed from heat.*

# Simple Curry Sauce
**Makes: 1½ cups**

 *A super simple curry sauce that goes with almost anything.*

400ml can coconut milk
1 tablespoon curry powder
1 teaspoon cornflour
1 tablespoon water

**Method:**
- Heat coconut milk in a saucepan over a low heat until hot *(not boiling).*
- Sprinkle over curry powder, mix well.
- Mix together cornflour and water until smooth. Gradually add to coconut milk, stirring over a medium heat until sauce boils and thickens. Season with salt and pepper.
- Add chopped vegies or your favourite ingredients.

# Cooking the Perfect Rice

*Cooking rice can be daunting at times. Cook smarter not harder and get yourself a rice cooker – it saves a lot of burnt rice. The higher-end ones can do more than just rice, but a simple rice cooker is all you need and they aren't expensive.*

- Use a rice cooker and your favourite white rice.
- Remove the bowl from your rice cooker, add rice and cover well with water, move and rub rice around with your hand until water becomes cloudy, then tip as much water out as you can without rice falling out.
- Repeat with at least 3 more lots of water or until water becomes clear.
- Add enough water to rice so when you place your index finger on top of rice the water comes up to the first line *(joint)* of your finger. *(Smooth the top of rice first with your hand so rice is level in bowl.)*
- Cover with lid and set to cook. Use a rice paddle or wooden spoon to fluff the rice when cooked.

# How to Cook the Perfect Steak

*Everyone has their own methods of cooking and how they like their steak done – this is what I do and works for me. The best way is to try different things, seasonings and methods, and see what works for you. Don't be afraid to get in and have a go.*

## How to:
• Season the steak with pepper up to 2 hours before, then with salt just before cooking.
• Heat a heavy–based frying pan until very hot but not smoking.
• Drizzle some oil into the pan and leave for a moment.
• Add the steak, a knob of butter, some garlic and robust, chopped herbs, if you want.
• Sear evenly on each side for recommended time *(see below)*, turning every minute for the best caramelised crust.
• Leave to rest on a board or warm plate for about 5 minutes.
• Serve steak whole or carved into slices with the resting juices poured over.

## What happens when you cook meat?
• When you cook meat the protein in it sets. Generally the softer it feels, the less cooked it is and vice versa. Cooking your steak to your liking is a skill that comes with time and a few overcooked dinners, too!
• While using a thermometer is accurate and takes the guesswork out of it, I feel there is something satisfying about being able to cook a steak perfectly by feel alone.

**I recommend the following for a 2cm thick sirloin steak:**
**Blue:** 1 minute each side
**Rare:** 1½ minutes each side
**Medium rare:** 2 minutes each side
**Medium:** About 2¼ minutes each side
**Medium–well:** About 3 to 4 minutes each side
**Well–done:** About 4 to 5 minutes each side

# How Long Should You Rest Your Beef?

*It really depends on the size and the cut of beef, but as a guide, bigger roasts should rest for 10 to 20 minutes and your steak should rest for at least 5 minutes. But experiment with what works the best and you'll be cooking mouth–watering, juicy steaks in no time.*

**What happens when you rest meat?**
- If you cut straight into your beautiful piece of steak after cooking it, it kind of defeats the purpose. The reason it needs to rest is because the juices need time to redistribute, otherwise they will just flow away, leaving you with a brown, but tougher and drier piece of meat.
- Another important thing to know is the residual heat will continue to cook your steak after you've removed it from the grill or the pan. So if your desired temperature is say 65°C, then it's best to remove the meat a few degrees south of this. It will come up to the desired temperature during the resting period, giving you a perfectly cooked steak.

# Other Kitchen Hacks

### Speedy meatloaf

When you've got a hankering for a hunka meat but don't want to wait an hour or more for the meatloaf to cook, then divide and conquer. Divvy the meat into individual portions in a muffin tin, and bake at 230°C for 15 minutes.

### Golden brown air fryer food

We love air fryers for giving us the crispy fried texture we love without the extra grease. However, air fryers don't always produce that golden hue we crave. You can fix that, though, with just a quick spritz of cooking oil spray before popping them into the air fryer basket. That very light coating of oil is all you need.

### Teach eggs to swim

Don't always rely on the date listed on your egg carton. How eggs have been stored can make a big difference to their freshness. A more accurate measure of age can be found flowing from your tap. Fill a tall glass or bowl with water, then carefully lower an egg inside. If it sinks and stays on the bottom, the egg is fresh. Even if it stands on one end, it's reasonably fresh. If it floats to the top *(a sign of air built up inside the shell)*, it's time to toss it.

### Easy measuring

Honey, maple syrup and other sticky ingredients slip right out of measuring cups when you grease them first. Spritz measuring cups and spoons with cooking oil spray before filling with the main event.

### Spiralizer curly fries

This twirly tool should not be reserved for zoodles alone. Spiralize a large potato or sweet potato, then toss with a tablespoon of oil and your favorite seasonings. Spread out evenly on a baking tray lined with baking paper and cook in oven at 210°C for about 20 minutes or until golden brown, stirring every 5 minutes to avoid burning any pieces.

### Leftover wine or stock

Don't dump the rest of that pinot or allow it to oxidize in the fridge for weeks on end. Pour leftover wine into an ice cube tray, top with plastic wrap to keep ice crystals at bay and freeze. Tomorrow, you'll have small portions that you can pop out and add to sauces, soups, risottos and stews for some almost instant depth of flavour.

### Use an egg slicer for fruits and vegies

This tiny kitchen tool isn't just for cutting hard–boiled eggs. It's great for cutting even portions of smaller fruits and vegies. Try slicing strawberries, kiwis and mushrooms into even thickness in one fell swoop (and without the finger–slicing risk of a mandoline).

### Make crispy hash browns in a waffle maker

Coarsely grate 6 medium desireee potatoes into a colander and use your hands to squeeze out as much excess liquid as possible. Mix together potato, 2 tablespoons plain flour, 1 egg and season with salt and pepper. Spoon potato mix in batches into a lightly greased waffle maker or a waffle iron and slam it shut. Cook until you get that crispy golden hash brown you are going for.

# Index

# Breakfast/Brunch

# Soups

## Pork

## Lamb

## Fish & Seafood

# Vegies & Salads

# Pasta & Bagettie

# Knockout Noodles & Rice

# Cakes & Extra Goodies

# After-School Snacks

# The Basics

# Acknowledgements

I'd like to thank everyone who helped me along this journey. Not in my wildest of dreams would I have thought I'd get this far! From uploading one video for giggles to being a published author is just crazy!

Many of you have guided and inspired me, whether it was just yarning about old times and the food we ate or joking around about ideas and letting sparks of creativity fly. I certainly could not have done it without your love, support and guidance.

A special shout out to my wife, my family and friends, the community, the Mob Feeds Facebook group, online inspiration, the Simon & Schuster team, my followers and all those who inspire me.